smart materials

axel ritter
smart materials
in architecture, interior architecture and design

Birkhäuser – Publishers for Architecture
Basel · Berlin · Boston

Phosphorescent ink, one of the smart materials mentioned in this book, has been used in the printing of the cover. The graphic reinterprets a 1970s wallpaper motif with an optical 3D-effect and at the same time resembles the molecular structure of a material. For more information on the effect of phosphorescence, which is particularly visible in a dark environment, see p. 118 ff.

Translation Raymond Peat, Alford

Graphic design, layout and cover Miriam Bussmann, Berlin

Cover idea, image research and selection Axel Ritter, Bad Neuenahr – Ahrweiler

Editor Andreas Müller, Berlin

Copyediting and proofreading Michael Wachholz, Berlin

This book is also available in a German language edition
(ISBN-13: 978-3-7643-7326-9, ISBN-10: 3-7643-7326-1).

A CIP catalogue record for this book is available from the Library of Congress, Washington D.C., USA

Bibliographic information published by Die Deutsche Bibliothek
Die Deutsche Bibliothek lists this publication in the Deutsche Nationalbibliografie; detailed bibliographic data is available in the Internet at <http://dnb.ddb.de>.

© 2007 Birkhäuser – Publishers for Architecture, P.O.Box 133, CH-4010 Basel, Switzerland
Part of Springer Science + Business Media
Printed on acid-free paper produced from chlorine-free pulp. TCF ∞
Printed in Germany

ISBN-13: 978-3-7643-7327-6
ISBN-10: 3-7643-7327-X

www.birkhauser.ch

9 8 7 6 5 4 3 2 1

contents

preface

"The whole is more than the sum of its parts."
(Aristotle, *384 BC)

This book is suitable for students, practitioners and teaching staff active in the fields of architecture, design and art: for all who are open to innovative technology, on the look out for new materials and products of use in the future or for those who just wish to be inspired. Criticism, suggestions and ideas relating to this publication are expressly welcomed. The author would be delighted to receive information about new materials at: info@ritter-architekten.com

The author has been involved in the development and application of smart materials and adaptive and kinetic structures in the fields of experimental architecture and innovative design for more than ten years. In addition to his activities as a freelance architect and designer, the author has published articles on the subject and presented invited lectures.

Time and time again utopians, futurologists and even some politicians have developed scenarios of how the world of tomorrow will look. In the past they have seldom been proved right. Much of what they foresaw just never happened as they said it would. In particular this applies to the timeframes envisaged, which are usually too brief, and to the frequent predictions for worldwide omnipresence of the phenomena.

Buildings and life in our buildings have changed over the last 25 years. Apart from a few exceptions, it is not spectacular buildings and housing types that define our times, it is above all the changes in building technology and automation. Through the development of innovative materials, products and constructions, the move to endow buildings with more functions, the desire for new means of expression, and ecological and economic constraints, it is now possible to design buildings that are clearly different from those of previous decades.

We are standing at the threshold of the next generation of buildings: buildings with various degrees of high technology, which are extremely ecological in their behaviour through the intelligent use of functionally adaptive materials, products and constructions and are able to react to changes in their direct or indirect surroundings and adjust themselves to suit.

This creates new tasks for the designers and planners of these buildings, who must ensure that, in achieving what is technically feasible, sight is not lost of the well-being of the occupants and they are given the opportunity of self-determination. To do this in the design process requires knowledge and integration of as many of these parameters as possible. The central role of technology and automation of processes must not lead to people being deprived of their right to make decisions; they must be given the opportunity to step in when the need arises to have things how they would like them.

That all too sensitive adaption processes are not always advantageous can be seen with the 1987 Institut du Monde Arabe (IMA) building in Paris by Jean Nouvel, which was fitted with a multitude of mechanical photo-shutters to control light transmission: people inside the building found the repeated adaption sequences a nuisance. They took place all the time, at short intervals and sometimes even under a heavily overcast sky. To cure the problem, the control was made less sensitive and the number of possible switching processes reduced.

Energy and matter flows can be optimised through the use of smart materials, as the majority of these materials and products take up energy and matter indirectly or directly from the environment. This approach does not entail any other related requirements, for example as would arise through conventionally networked automation products. Currently the use of smart material is made necessary by the wish for more automation, for compact materials and products reacting to sensors and actuators and the increasing global demand on expensive energy sources and raw materials.

Depending on the future popularity of use of smart materials and the visible effects on our buildings, our picture in relation to our built environment will change from what we are used to seeing as architecture. Metropolises like Tokyo, which is undergoing a continuous and rapid change of appearance in some districts, show that people are capable of living with permanent architectural change.

With special thanks to:

The publisher

and the following people
Dr. Alexander Kraft, Dr. Karl-Heinz Heckner,
Gesimat GmbH, Berlin, Germany
Dr. Arno Seeboth, Fraunhofer Institut für Angewandte
Polymerforschung (IAP), Potsdam-Golm, Germany
Prof. Christina Kubisch, Hoppegarten, Germany
Erhard Klein, Galerie Klein, Bad Münstereifel,
Germany
Eun Sook Lee, Korea
Dr. Gerhard Span, SAM – Span and Mayrhofer KEG,
Wattens, Austria
Dr. Hartmut Schubert, OKER-Chemie GmbH, Germany
Prof. Dr. Norbert Hampp, Philipps-Universität,
Marburg, Germany
Dipl. Masch.-Ing. ETH Patrick Lochmatter, Eidge-
nössische Materialprüfungs-und Forschungsanstalt
(EMPA), Dübendorf, Switzerland
Ruth Handschin, Zürich, Switzerland

and the following companies
Deutsche Steinzeug Cremer & Breuer AG,
Schwarzenfeld, Germany
G.B.C. Ltd., Oxfordshire, England
James Robinson Ltd., Huddersfield, England
Micropelt GmbH, Freiburg, Germany
Novaled AG, Dresden, Germany
PI Ceramic GmbH, Lederhose, Germany
Prinz Optics GmbH, Stromberg, Germany
Taiyo Europe GmbH, Munich, Germany

Smart materials is a relatively new term for materials and products that have changeable properties and are able to reversibly change their shape or colour in response to physical and/or chemical influences, e.g. light, temperature or the application of an electric field. Non-smart materials have no such special properties, semi-smart materials are notable for their ability, for example, to change their shape in response to an influence once or a few times. With smart materials these changes are repeatable and reversible.

Semi-smart materials and smart materials are what we might call functional materials. The term "material", as it is used here, includes substances from which intermediate products can be made, as well as the generic materials themselves. The terms "interior architecture" and "architecture" have been used in places but elsewhere "architecture" can be read to cover both.

Smart materials are often described as adaptive or intelligent materials. Whilst most of the smart materials known today may also be described as adaptive materials because of their property to adjust themselves, the description "intelligent materials" is to be considered as colloquial. This description is incorrect as intelligence also has associations with computer science, and the materials and products known to date are not generally suitable or until now have not been used in such a context.

A change in one property of smart materials may often be accompanied by changes in other properties. Certain photochromic compounds (PC) change colour reversibly in response to light and to temperature changes. And inversely it may be the case that several properties change at once after stimulation by a single influence. For example, magnetorheologic fluids (MRF) under the influence of a magnetic field, in addition to changing their flow properties, also change the electrical, thermal, acoustic and optical properties of their suspensions at the same time. Some smart materials also exhibit the inverse behaviour by making changes in both directions. Piezoelectric smart materials are able to generate electric charges from the effect of compression or tension and in reverse change their shape on application of an electric field. It is occasionally possible to combine several materials or products with smart properties together to create complex change behaviours.

The use of materials with changing properties is not an invention of modern times. From earliest history man has poured hot water over wood to induce it to swell and split rock. Pine cones, intestines and long blonde human hair have been used to indicate moisture in the air and as actuators in air humidly gauges. The change in length of two different metals joined to one another was used from the beginning of the industrial revolution in thermoelectric switches.

The following physical and chemical influencing variables may act as triggering stimuli for changes in smart materials:

LIGHT, UV LIGHT
The visible and ultraviolet part of electromagnetic radiation.
TEMPERATURE
The thermal state of a physical system, e.g. a body.
PRESSURE
The ratio of force to area.
ELECTRIC FIELD
The field in the vicinity of an electric charge.
MAGNETIC FIELD
The field in the vicinity of a magnet or moving electrical charge, e.g. a wire carrying an electric current.
CHEMICAL ENVIRONMENT
The presence of certain chemical elements and/or compounds, e.g. water.

The chapter on trends and developments introduces the subject and gives a first look into fields other than architecture, whilst innovative materials and products give an overview of current developments in material research and product development. In order to make the distinction they are compared with other innovative non- and semi-smart materials.

The main part of the book deals with the different types of smart materials, using descriptions comprising combinations of adjectives mainly from the Greek. For example, an influence such as light has been expressed as "photo" and a changing property such as colour as "chromic". In the above case the full description is "photochromic smart materials". The illustrations and legends are normally referred to from top left to bottom and then from top right to bottom. The illustrations in the introduction to the individual groups of smart materials are normally taken from the projects presented in the respective group.

In the sequence and division of the smart materials shown here some special points had to be taken into account. Classification in accordance with influencing factors and changing properties does not make things absolutely clear, as with some smart materials changes may be triggered by two, three or more different influences or in other cases stimulation by a single influence can result in several properties changing at the same time. Therefore the materials have been differentiated on a case by case basis from the point of view of their importance in the context of realised or future architectural applications. The materials chosen offer an overview of the smart materials most suitable at the current time for use in architecture, interior architecture and design.

trends and developments

ARCHITECTURE

Trends and developments emerge at different rates in the field of architecture, depending on the commercial and political conditions, geographic location, natural-anthropogenic environment, and technological and financial possibilities. Innovative materials have a recurring and crucial role to play here.

Hybrid Muscle with harnessed white buffalo: R&Sie... architects. | View from outside. | Interior view.

ecological architecture

Materials and products used in this field include those that can be recycled or are manufactured from waste. In many cases this is at the developer's own risk, as usually no construction approval has been granted. Fire safety or toxicity or both are often the main concerns that make it more difficult for these materials and products to become established in normal use.

An example of how a building can transform mechanical energy into electrical energy is the project *Hybrid Muscle* by the French architects R&Sie...: a 3t counterweight placed in a building was raised by a white buffalo and provided enough electricity from a dynamo-electric generator for the lighting, a laptop and a telephone system.

There are also a few instances where the energy comes from humans, for example by converting their movements into electrical energy; this could be during sport or whilst walking. A current interpretation along the lines of this theme is provided by the architect Mitchell Joachim with his idea of a floating fitness studio. The sporting muscle power of the people using the gym is converted by suitable means into electrical energy and used to drive the *RiverGym NY*, which – sheltered against the weather by a transparent protective cupola – is able to change its surroundings again and again.

Two works by the author, *Dynaf l e x p01* and *Anthrogena*, show that energy obtained from people can be used directly to change the geometry of architectonic space in a purely mechanical way. *Dynaf l e x p01* is a weight-controlled load-bearing structure, which increases in length in response to the vertical deflection of parts of the structure, caused by people walking over it (see electricity-generating smart materials, pp. 162 ff. [1]). By contrast, in *Anthrogena*, in addition to spreading in width in response to load, the structure deforms and is stabilised by the transfer of volumes of air.

non-changeable/non-changing architecture

Depending on their geographical and topographic location, buildings are subject to and must sometimes be protected from various atmospheric, local and anthropological influences. Self-cleaning materials have been developed for this purpose and are incorporated into building elements such as roof tiles, membranes and into facades in order to keep them permanently clean. Self-healing coatings and seals have been developed that reseal themselves in the event of damage to restore their protective effect and make costly repairs unnecessary. Highly resistant materials and coatings are also being developed, for example using nanometre-scale particles, to create surfaces with particularly high scratch-, fracture- or heat-resistance (see p. 42 and titaniumdioxide (TiO_2), pp. 100 ff.). These developments are of particular interest for buildings that have to withstand extreme climatic conditions and/or are expected to remain in use for a very long time.

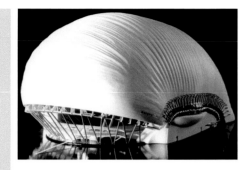

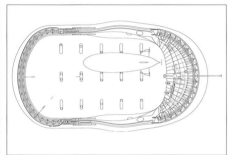

Airship hangar *Morphyt nt* in the closed state, rear view. | Plan of hangar. | View from above of a model of the weight-controlled load-bearing structure *Anthrogena*. | Side view. | *RiverGym NY* in action. | Several *RiverGyms NY* on the New York skyline.

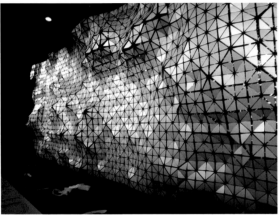

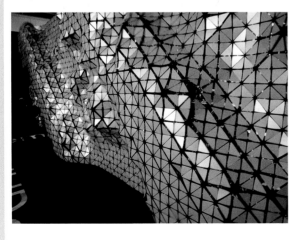

changeable/changing architecture

Architecture can be designed to change or be changed in specific ways. Instead of tolerating or counteracting involuntary changes in buildings caused by natural and/or anthropological influences, some architects are seeking to use these effects as a formal element in their projects. In recent years more work has been done on so-called adaptive building envelopes, which, in the ideal case, are able to react to their immediate and adjacent surroundings in a manner quite unlike earlier structures. Depending on their design and sensory systems, and their passive and active structures and components, they are able to react reversibly to their surroundings over a long period of time. This task requires materials and products with reversible properties.

Property-determining parameters relevant to architecture that can be designed as changing or changeable include:

SHAPE	COLOUR/APPEARANCE	SOUND (NOISE)	ODOUR (SCENT)

SHAPE

For various reasons it may be worthwhile and helpful for the shape of a part or the whole of a building to have the capacity of being changed or changing itself. So-called convertible roofs, i.e. roofs capable of folding or with sections that slide over one another, and consisting of stiff and/or flexible surface-forming constructions, have been increasingly used since the 1970s as temporary weather protection in the form of roofing for stadia or swimming pools. An innovative concept for a pneumatically convertible roof was developed by the author as part of a design for an airship hangar in which the hangar was covered with a bivalent load-bearing structure consisting of a three-layer inflatable membrane. When the hangar is closed, a slight overpressure stabilises the building skin, using the principle of a pneumatic structure. To open the hangar, air is introduced into the initially flat voids in the membrane so that the inflated voids become pressurised arches to take over the load-bearing role. The contraction of the hangar skin on filling with air opens the gate.

US-American dECOi Architects developed an interactive kinetic wall, the Aegis Hyposurface. A number of pneumatic reactive actuators were built into a basic structural frame. The actuators were mechanically connected to a surface made up of rows of diagonally divided, movable tiles on the outside of the structure. The wall reacts to various stimuli such as light, sound and movement. Special software causes the surface to change spatially. The spontaneous movements of the tiles give an almost natural-looking simulation of moving waves, among other effects.

Aegis Hyposurface in action. | *opposite: CycleBowl*

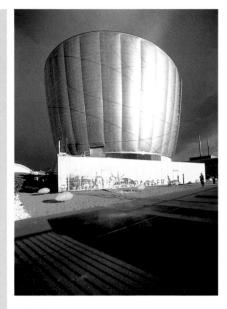

COLOUR/APPEARANCE

Relatively high cost and inadequate long-term stability mean that self-acting colour-changing materials are still seldom used for external surfaces. The situation is different inside buildings, where there have already been a number of different applications; these are described in more detail in the sections below.

Optically switchable layers in building envelopes can be designed to provide both a temporary privacy screen and controlled darkening of a room. In addition to specifically sensitive materials that switch from opaque to transparent at certain temperatures or when an electric field is applied, there have also been various mechanical systems developed in the past. One system capable of exerting a varying influence on the transparency of the outside skin of a building is the ETFE film wall of the *CycleBowl*, which architects Atelier Brückner of Stuttgart, Germany, developed for Expo 2000 in Hanover. The triple-layer pillows each comprise three sheets; one with a positive print, one with a negative print and one left transparent. Under pneumatic control the printed middle sheet could be pressed against the reverse-printed outer sheet or against the unprinted inner sheet to make the facade appear flat at certain times and three-dimensional at others. Furthermore, the internal space could also be sealed overhead against sunlight by pneumatically controlled inflatable tubes integrated in the roof.

SOUND (NOISE)

There are attempts to make constructional elements such as walls and windows sound-insulative by the active superimposition of sound waves. An arriving sound wave is analysed and then neutralised by the sending out of an opposite sound wave. For this a piezoelectric sound converter can be used (see piezoelectric ceramics/polymers, pp. 154 ff.).

ODOUR (SCENT)

Manufacturers in China have succeeded in developing materials with embedded scents, which, when used as floor coverings and walked on, are able to release scent molecules into the room air. An accessible sculpture with an external skin consisting completely of rows of potted fragrant plants was created by Danish/Icelandic-born but German-domiciled artist Olafur Eliasson in his work *Dufttunnel* for the "Car City" in Wolfsburg 2004. The three linked tunnel sections are kept continuously rotating to adequately supply the plants with natural light and to intensify the effect of the scent. The fragrant plants are replaced every six weeks with new ones during the period of display in the summer months of April to September.

A further possibility for using odours in architecture is in the area of perfume marketing.

CycleBowl | *Dufttunnel* at the "Car City" in Wolfsburg.

intelligent architecture

The *TRON Intelligent House*, the first building we would consider intelligent by today's standards, was designed in 1988 by Ken Sakamura in Nishi Azuba, Japan. Costing 1 billion yen at that time, the fully automated building contained a total of 380 computers, which were networked with the TRON architecture. All external information received, for example, from television, radio and telephone, and all internal information, exchanged for example via an audiovisual system, could be called up on monitors installed in every room.

Ten years later in 1998, Bill Gates had a smart house built, which, with the help of integral sensors and associated software, is capable of recognising people and, depending on user preferences, produces a change in the environment, so that, for example, when a person enters a room a favourite image is displayed on a monitor.

A consortium of several Fraunhofer Institutes and private companies coordinated by the Fraunhofer Institute for Microelectronic Circuits and Systems (IMS) developed the *InHaus*, which was erected in 2001 in Duisburg, Germany. In addition to developing and networking the technical equipment, the project's purpose is the integration of this equipment into a modern-home aesthetic, ergonomy, comfort and lifestyle. The SmarterWohnenNRW initiative, which is currently Europe's largest active smart-living project, will create 1000 pilot homes in North Rhine-Westphalia, again with the participation of several Fraunhofer Institutes.

In principle, intelligent buildings can also be created through the use of smart materials. These buildings would require structures capable of receiving and processing a multitude of complex data, preferably involving electrical systems. If such a structure remains dependent on a simple matter of stimulus and reaction, then a system cannot be described as intelligent.

decorative architecture

Decorative elements can take on other functions, for example in order to achieve weight reduction or to allow views into a space by removing the negative form from a surface. Further functions are those of solar protection or a privacy screen, often in the form of printed or sandblasted glass surfaces. In this context there are a number of different effects that can be created by the use of new types of colour-changing and optically switchable materials and products. For example, initially severe-looking, monochrome surfaces can be suddenly enlivened by the effect of certain stimuli. This may be through the use of a transparent, moisture-sensitive paint applied over certain areas to reveal a pattern when rain falls upon it.

One such use is demonstrated by the author's 1995 work *hydrophil-hydrophob*. By applying a liquid, silicone-based, transparent dampproofing agent to certain parts of two cast-stone panels, it was possible to produce the desired contrasting light-dark effect.

hydrophil-hydrophob II (2006) before and after the effect of water.

DESIGN AND ART

Textiles, automobiles and furniture have to satisfy high requirements before they enter series production. However, new, innovative materials and products can sometimes be introduced more quickly in these industries than in architecture, and even more so than in the construction fields. In certain circumstances, materials and products tested in these other fields can also be modified to be used in architectural applications. It is not unusual for artists, with their sensitivity and pleasure in experimentation, to be the first to use innovative materials and products, and develop some unusual applications for them.

textile design

In earlier times textiles generally had only one or two permanent properties. Today more and more textiles with changing properties are being developed, i.e. they can change themselves in response to one or more influencing factors. This is made possible by materials and their products with inherent self-changing properties, so-called smart materials. These smart materials may be already available, newly introduced on to the market, or they may be newly developed products. They can be used on their own or in combination with non-smart or semi-smart materials.

The following section deals with textile design only in relation to clothing, as textiles used for architectural purposes are described in the main part of this book.

In addition to numerous experimental design projects, recent years have seen the emergence of various textile materials in functional clothing, including so-called intelligent clothing. Some examples of clothing, already available or at the prototype stage, reflecting these trends in which smart materials play a major role are described below. Some of their properties and special qualities can also be used for architectural purposes, be it in the form described here or in a different modification.

DIRT-REPELLENT CLOTHING INCORPORATING NANOPARTICLES
SEMI-SMART MATERIALS

To protect suits from water or stubborn stains such as ketchup and coffee, Bugatti, a German manufacturer of high-priced men's clothing, made them from a special fabric that disposes of dirt by means of a self-cleaning effect due to incorporated nanometre-scale particles.

SHAPE-CHANGING CLOTHING INCORPORATING SHAPE-MEMORY ALLOY (SMA)
SMART MATERIALS

The Italian clothing company Corpo Nove, through its spin-off firm Grado Zero Espace, manufactured a long-sleeved shirt out of a fabric incorporating a shape-memory alloy (SMA), in this case, Nitinol. Depending on how it has been preprogrammed, the fabric forms itself into different shapes in response to the ambient temperature. The shirt with the name *Oricalco* rolls up its own sleeves. When the room temperature exceeds a certain value, the fabric in the sleeves forms folds and the sleeves shorten in length. The shirt can also be compressed into its smallest possible volume, for example for transport. By allowing it to reach a preprogrammed temperature, e.g. by the introduction of warm air from a hairdryer, it regains its original shape.

Self-cleaning suits for men. | *opposite: Oricalco* shirt: complete view. | Folding shortens the sleeves. | Close-up photograph of the textile.

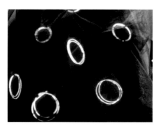

COLOUR-CHANGING CLOTHING WITH THERMOCHROMIC DYES
SMART MATERIALS

Founded in Italy as an interactive design consultancy and research laboratory, Cute Circuit has developed and manufactured several changeable clothing textiles, including the skirt *Skirteleon*, which can change its colour and pattern depending on the activities and mood of the person wearing it. In the morning at work, the skirt is blue; by late afternoon, for example when meeting friends, an animal motif appears; and in the evening at a restaurant it takes on an elegant Japanese pattern.

LIGHT-EMITTING CLOTHING INCORPORATING ELECTROLUMINESCENT CABLE (EL CABLE)
SMART MATERIALS

Cute Circuit's black, Victorian-inspired *KineticDress* reacts to the physical activity of the wearer. It has a pattern of electroluminescent rings that respond to the intensity of body movements by emitting different intensities of light. When the wearer is involved in peaceful activities such as reading, the garment looks black. Leisurely movement, such as walking, produces slightly illuminated blue rings. With more strenuous movement, such as dancing, the rings become fully illuminated.

CLIMATE-REGULATING CLOTHING INCORPORATING SHAPE-MEMORY POLYMER (SMA)
SMART MATERIALS

Another product from Grado Zero Espace is a leather jacket with several functional layers. The application of ordinary cigarette paper to the leather enables the leather itself to be kept extremely thin. The jacket also has a moisture- and heat-regulating climatic membrane made from a shape-memory polymer (SMP), which controls the permeability to perspiration and flow of heat, in response to body temperature. A serious search for architectonic uses of SMPs is currently underway.

CLIMATE-REGULATING CLOTHING INCORPORATING PELTIER ELEMENTS (PE)
SMART MATERIALS

The same company also developed actively cooling underclothes for racing car drivers. The underwear incorporates Peltier elements (PE), which can be constructed like thermoelectric generators (TEG) (see themoelectric generators (TEG), pp. 148 ff.), but unlike TEGs they are able to convert electric current into heat and cold. A similar actively cooling textile was developed at the University of Minho in Portugal. Here as well, the cooling effect is based on thermoelectric conversion.

Skirteleon skirt: close-up photograph of the textile with the animal motif visible. | *KineticDress* during various activities. | Close-up photo-graph of the textile with illuminated rings made from EL cables.

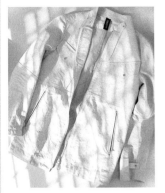

SCENT-CHANGING CLOTHING INCORPORATING CYCLODEXTRINS
SEMI-SMART MATERIALS

To prevent the build-up of odour, fabrics for certain suits made by Bugatti, Germany, incorporate non-toxic naturally absorbent cyclodextrins, which take up smoke, sweat or fat in their hydrophobic hollow interiors.

SUPERINSULATIVE CLOTHING INCORPORATING AEROGEL
NON-SMART MATERIALS

For extreme cold, Corpo Nove designed the *Absolute Frontier* jacket, which uses the thermally insulative material aerogel. Developed already in 1930, aerogel is the best heat-insulative material available on the market, second only to vacuumised products. In the near future we could see clothing only 3 mm thick being adequately insulative down to –50°C. Aerogel is also used in architecture, for example as a heat-insulative material between glass panes.

DEFENSIVE CLOTHING WITH ELECTRON-EMITTING TEXTILES AND LEDs
SMART MATERIALS

The *No-Contact* jacket designed by the US-American company of the same name is intended to defend the wearer against attack. Primarily marketed for the protection of women, the wearer first activates the jacket with a key. An LED lets the wearer know this has been done. In the event of an attack, the wearer presses a control button in either of the sleeves to release a pulsating electrical current of low amperage but at a voltage of 80,000 volts, which flows through the surface of the jacket. The jacket creates visual and audible electric arcs between the shoulders and collar to warn off an approaching attacker.

COMMUNICATING CLOTHING WITH INTEGRATED MP3 PLAYER
SEMI-SMART MATERIALS

A jacket with an integrated MP3 player has been developed by Infineon in conjunction with system partners. This is an example of so-called wearable electronics. Earlier electronic components could not be fully integrated into clothing because they would be rendered non-functional by washing. Here the company developed a solution in which all four components (audio-chip, power module, microphone and controls) of the system were fully encapsulated to protect them against moisture, and had high-quality, adequately resistant seals. Fine wires were woven into the fabric to transfer the electrical signals. The power was supplied at first from lithium-ion polymer rechargeable batteries, which in the later series production phase would be replaced by thermogenerator chips (see thermoelectric generators (TEG), pp. 148 ff.). These chips would generate an electric current with an output of more than 1.0 µW/cm and a voltage of 5 V/cm from the small temperature difference between skin and clothing. In most cases this is adequate for low power components such as sensors and microchips. However, up to now no products incorporating thermogenerator chips have been brought on to the market.

Jacket with moisture- and heat-regulating climate membrane. | Actively cooling T-shirt. | *Absolute Frontier* jacket. | *No-contact* jacket.

COMMUNICATING CLOTHING INCORPORATING BLUETOOTH TECHNOLOGY
SEMI-SMART MATERIALS

One suitable technology for communicating over a distance is Bluetooth, which Cute Circuit from Italy incorporated in its 2004 *F+R Hugs* shirt system in order to transmit data about contact events. The system, already available today, consists of a shirt equipped with Bluetooth, sensors and actuators, a mobile phone and special software. Contact with the appropriately coloured sensitive areas on the shirt creates electric voltages; these are picked up by the system's mobile telephone and transmitted by radio, in the form of electromagnetic waves, to the mobile telephone partner of the wearer's choice; there again they are converted, by activation of the actuators in the partner's shirt, into similar movements.

LIGHT-EMITTING HANDBAG INCORPORATING ELECTROLUMINESCENT FILM (EL FILM)
SMART MATERIALS

The German company BREE produced a handbag with an interior light consisting of a three-dimensional, deformable luminescent film (EL film), which was developed by Bayer, Germany, and a Swiss electronics specialist. The uniform level of light emitted over an area lights up the full interior of the handbag.

F+R Hugs shirt system | Handbag with activated EL film fitted on the side: views from outside and into the bag. | Jacket with integrated MP3 player and other electronic components.

automobile design

Automobile design, which has distinguished itself time and time again through particularly innovative, sometimes spectacular developments, can take the credit for a number of new smart materials worthwhile mentioning that could also be of interest for architectural applications. Various prototypes and series production vehicles in which smart materials have been used and innovative concepts realised are described below.

**COLOUR-, SOUND- AND SCENT-CHANGING AUTOMOBILE WITH
ELECTROLUMINESCENT FILMS (EL FILMS) AND SCENT GENERATOR**
SMART MATERIALS

An automobile with a number of sensory abilities was developed by the Swiss design and concept powerhouse Rinspeed in conjunction with several system partners. The *Senso* model, presented at the 2005 motor show in Geneva, has a system for detecting and influencing the emotional state of the driver. The positive stimuli emanating from the vehicle are intended to make the driver drive more safely. The automobile has a biometric watch, which measures the driver's pulse, and a mobile eye camera, which records his driving behaviour. An onboard computer evaluates the collected data and offers the driver different visual, acoustic and olfactory stimuli, depending on his current state of mind: a total of four LCD monitors and interior finishes which can be illuminated in different colours create orange light to excite, blue to calm and green patterns for the evenly balanced state. The interior finishes are made from electroluminescent films (EL films) and give off a uniform area light. As smart surface technology this was their first application in an automobile (see thick film electroluminescence/electroluminescent materials (EL), pp. 130 ff.); specially composed tones are played as acoustic support to the driver and scents are released through the vehicle ventilation system, either an invigorating citrus-grapefruit or a calming vanilla-mandarin (see p. 41).

OPTICALLY CHANGING AUTOMOBILE WITH ELECTROOPTICAL COMPONENTS
SMART MATERIALS

In the luxury model class, the *Maybach 62* has the option of being fitted with an integral electrotransparent panoramic roof, which switches reversibly between transparent and opaque to provide solar protection or to darken the interior.

SCENT-CHANGING AUTOMOBILE WITH SCENT GENERATOR
SEMI-SMART MATERIALS

A sophisticated scent concept was developed as part of a study for an estate version of the Mini, the *Mini Concept*, which now has been built into a number of variants: a monitor mounted centrally on the dashboard can display a number of different driving scenarios, each associated with a specific scent. A device in the engine compartment introduces the scent into the vehicle interior through a ventilation outlet on the driver's side.

Senso: colour changes possible with EL films. | *Maybach 62:* the integral electrotransparent panoramic roof viewed from the inside. | *Mini Concept:* view of the dashboard and the scent outlet nozzle integrated into the A-pillar.

furniture design

As furniture used inside rooms is exposed to no or only slightly demanding climatic conditions, much less expensive materials and products can be used.

COLOUR-CHANGING FURNITURE WITH THERMOCHROMIC DYES
SMART MATERIALS

Colour-changing furniture is relatively easy to produce by using textiles with the appropriate properties. In the two chairs *tictac*, a work designed and implemented at the Interactive Institute in Sweden as part of the STATIC! project, the top surfaces used for depositing items are equipped with violet and red temperature-sensitive colour-changing fabric. At normal room temperatures the surface is monochrome, whilst above a certain temperature, depending on the thermochromic components used, a colour change occurs. This could be caused by contact with hot surfaces or by warm room air.

LIGHT-EMITTING FURNITURE INCORPORATING PHOSPHORESCENT GLAZE
SMART MATERIALS

Glass tables that luminesce in the dark have been developed by the interior and product designers Gruppe RE, based in Cologne, Germany. A top coat of phosphorescent glass-ceramic paint stores daylight and artificial light and releases it again in darkness. The top coat, which can be applied by a number of different processes including screen printing, is baked to create a strong bond between the glaze and the glass surface.

LIGHT-EMITTING FURNITURE INCORPORATING LUMINATING FABRIC
SEMI-SMART MATERIALS

The Italian company Luminex has a luminating textile in its range of products. It is a composite fabric made from conventional threads and light-conducting threads, and can be illuminated in different colours. Artificially created light is conducted to each separate thread end of the light-conducting part of the fabric and reflected at the inner surfaces so that the major proportion of light is re-emitted. One possible use for these luminating textiles could be as covering for seats.

tictac chairs, with areas of colour change.

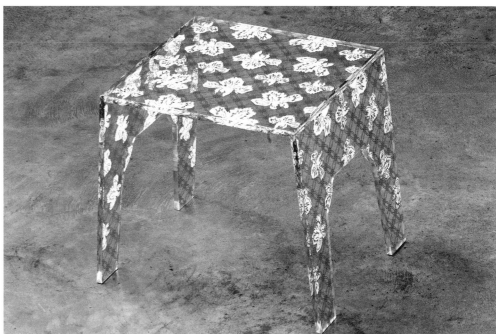

Seats with different colours of luminating light-conducting fabrics. | Luminescent glass table by day and at night.

Hygrowall: right half of the conch with applied hygro-/hydrochromic paint in the unsaturated state (lavender-blue) and the almost saturated state (rose-red). | *opposite: Tips:* overall view by day and at night. | Close-up photograph by day and at night.

art

There are many instances of the use of special, new and innovative materials, products and smart material applications in the field of art. It is not unusual for artists, with their sensitivity, their feeling for social issues, individual analysis and pleasure in experimentation, to search out interesting methods of expression not previously exploited.

COLOUR-CHANGING ART USING SILVER NITRATE
SEMI-SMART MATERIALS

By the start of the 1970s, the German artist Sigmar Polke was already experimenting and painting with materials that were capable of changing themselves. In several of his earlier pictures he used various photographic materials such as light-sensitive silver nitrate, which turns black over time when subjected to light. This process was not reversible. For Polke the autonomous creation of these pictures was an interesting phenomenon, because he could not foresee at the outset what the final effects would be (after [2]). In addition to non-reversible silver nitrate the artist also experimented with reversible, temperature- (see thermochromic/-tropic materials (TC, TT) p. 80) and moisture-sensitive paints.

COLOUR-CHANGING ART USING COBALT CHLORIDE PAINTS
SMART MATERIALS

For the XLII Biennale in Venice, Italy, in 1986, Polke covered the inside of the conch on the pavilion of the Federal Republic of Germany with a hygro-/hydrochromic paint consisting of a water-bound cobalt chloride solution. The paint changed its colour, depending on the degree of air humidity, from lavender-blue (unsaturated state) through purple and rose-red on to red (saturated state).

LIGHT-EMITTING ART USING PHOSPHORESCENT PAINT
SMART MATERIALS

The *Schattenwand mit Blitzelektronik* completed by the German artist Konrad Lueg in 1968 is a very early artistic work in which phosphorescent paint was used. When triggered by a flashgun, the three-part, 200 cm x 341.50 cm screen was excited and phosphoresced. If objects or people passed between the screen and the flashgun, they would remain as shadows for a moment.

Phosphorescent materials still inspire a great number of artists to use them for paintings and installations. Phosphorescent paints do not always have to be applied over the whole of a surface. This is shown by the installation *Tips*, set up in 1998 by the New York artist Sharon Louden. For her installation, Louden used steel wire to weave an enormous number of suitably treated dental cotton plugs into a three-dimensional carpet-like texture, an idea that could conceivably be adapted into a facade design. Under light, the 150 cm x 400 cm installation looks like a soft, white carpet with yellowish and black inclusions; in the dark the black parts disappear and the impression is one of a luminating meadow.

innovative materials and products

There are a great number of materials and products currently being developed that are close to market introduction or already available. Some have been developed specifically for use in the field of architecture; others were originally intended for use in product design, e.g. in textiles or automobiles, and are only offered to architects sporadically or not at all through their usual product suppliers. If architects are in the position to incorporate these materials and products directly or in modified form into their works, then a flood of new, interesting possibilities for building design and construction can ensue. Creative architects especially develop their own innovative materials and products for specific applications, or they develop new applications and the associated materials and products, which they subsequently arrange to have manufactured. Thus not infrequently the architect may be the designer, developer and manufacturer.

Depending on their characteristics, their structure and other properties, materials and substances today can be generally differentiated as follows:

RECYCLABLE MATERIALS
These materials are manufactured mainly from crushed and cleaned waste. Unless the raw material is sorted in advance to separate out the valuable fractions, the resulting products are usually of lower quality than the originally used materials.
BIODEGRADABLE MATERIALS
Materials, e.g. from vegetable starches, that are decomposed and completely broken down by microorganisms living in the soil.
BIOMATERIALS
Plastics and other materials made from renewable sources. One current research focus, for example, is the use of special CO_2-consuming bacteria in the production of biodegradable plastics.
NONVARIABLE MATERIALS
These materials are largely unaffected by physical and chemical influences, e.g. changes in ambient temperatures. One such material is the metal alloy Invar.
FUNCTIONAL SUBSTANCES
A general term for monofunctional and multifunctional substances.
SMART MATERIALS
Belong to the functional substances. These materials, substances and products have changeable properties and are able to reversibly change their shape or colour in response to physical and/or chemical influences, e.g. light, temperature or the application of an electrical field. They can be differentiated into non-smart materials, semi-smart materials and smart materials.
HYBRID MATERIALS
These materials are manufactured by combining at least two different components, e.g. biological with synthetic components.
FUNCTIONALLY GRADIENT MATERIALS
Composite materials with gradually merging layers. This results in a continuous change in material properties.
NANOMATERIALS
Materials made from nanometre-scale substances. They can be used as coatings or in product manufacture, for example.

The following section highlights several recent trends in materials and products, some of which are of particular interest in the field of architecture but at times also in other areas of design activity such as product design, for example.

durable materials and products

One approach to making buildings insensitive to certain external influences, for example so that they can withstand extreme conditions, is to use particularly durable (resistant) materials and products. Another approach is to use materials and products, at times even constructions, that are able to repair themselves, change their functions or strengthen themselves. Examples of such materials and products include:

DURABLE (RESISTANT) NON- AND SEMI-SMART MATERIALS

One example is spider silk, a material that above all is associated with future textiles and distinguishes itself by special elasticity and strength. After decades of research it is now capable of being manufactured synthetically in adequate quality and in large, i.e. economically viable, quantities. Canadian and US-American scientists were the first to succeed in isolating spider genes and inserting them into cells from hamsters and cows. Nowadays goats are used whose milk yields synthetic spider protein. Marketed under the commercial name of Biosteel, one of the uses of this silk is in bullet-proof vests. The manufacture of synthetic spider threads in large bioreactors can be traced back to a German research team who first identified and transferred the spider gene, so important to the production of silk, into bacterial cells. In addition to the use of artificially created silk in textiles, applications in the fields of paper and construction materials are being tested; here silk could be used as reinforcement. It would be conceivable to construct impact- or bullet-proof textile building envelopes, for example, to be used as roofs for sporting arenas and other structures.

SELF-HEALING NON- AND SEMI-SMART MATERIALS

As this is a relatively young area of research, there are only a few materials and products available with this function. The great potential for use of these products and the anticipated economic success mean that work on new and further developments is ongoing in many different industries.

Depending on reusability and reproducibility, there are systems in which the self-healing processes may be reversible or non-reversible.

Self-healing non-smart materials, for example geotextiles with bentonite (see mineral ad-/absorbents (MAd, MAb), pp. 175 ff.) can be classed as smart materials and will be dealt with in the main section of this book. Here only systems with limited smart properties will be discussed. A good example are the self-healing plastics that are being developed at the University of Illinois (UIUC), USA. The system is described by the university's researchers as an "autonomic healing system" or "self-healing system". It consists of a shape-giving epoxy polymer matrix, in which evenly distributed catalysts and microcapsules filled with a healing medium are embedded. If a break in the epoxy polymer occurs, the healing medium contained in the microcapsules that have been fractured is released and the site of the break is filled. Contact with the catalyst results in polymerisation: the fracture is then permanently sealed.

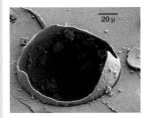

Self-healing paint is especially interesting to the automobile industry because with this system tiny scratches, such as those occuring during a visit to the car wash or off-road driving, are automatically sealed. To achieve this, a highly elastic resin is used, which spreads itself out evenly over the surface and seals small holes. The first production line use of such a paint has recently been implemented by a Japanese automobile manufacturer on an off-road vehicle. In the near future the use of this material is likely to be extended to scratch-prone items such as external mirrors and bumpers.

In architecture it would be possible to use such materials for example for high-gloss surfaces in handrail and baseboard areas where only slight scratch damage is expected and complete painted surfaces are desired, but have not been feasible so far.

Many people are unaware of the fact that one of the reasons historic structures such as Roman aqueducts or Gothic churches have lasted so long are the inherent self-healing properties of the binder used. This self-healing effect is evident in one particular 18th century bridge in Amsterdam; here water dissolves out the calcite from the porous clay bricks and transports it into any cracks, where it permanently seals them [3]. The so-called self-healing concretes today have fibres added to them that break at a particular load and release an effective filler. A new approach presently being examined at the Delft University of Technology, Netherlands, is the addition of calcite-forming bacteria to concrete.

SELF-REINFORCING NON- AND SEMI-SMART MATERIALS

A relatively new area of research is examining the possibilities of materials with self-reinforcing properties, which could also be of interest for future building construction. For example, the Technical University of Clausthal, Germany, has carried out research on self-reinforcing polymers based on polypropylene (PP). The researchers found out that "an axially strained PP, surrounded by a readily flowable PP to form a two-component PP, exhibits a different behaviour when strained or subjected to temperature effects" compared with ordinary polymers [4].

Technology by UIUC: schematic representation of the construction and functioning of the "autonomic healing system". | Specially shaped material sample for test purposes. | SEM photograph of a broken microcapsule. | Close-up photograph of the "autonomic healing system." | Embedded microcapsules.

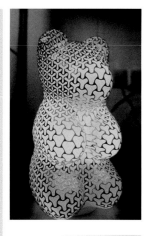
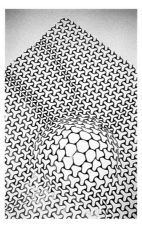

changeable/changing materials and products

Sensitive and reactive materials, products and constructions are required to help buildings react dynamically to various influences for reasons of stability and energy absorption, for example. Variable/changing materials and products can be of use in this context. They are capable of changing their properties themselves or their properties being changed by external influences such as the effect of light, temperature, force and/or the application of an electrical field. These influences may lead to changes directly without conversion, or indirectly with conversion. For example, a force may, without conversion into any other form of energy, produce reversible plastic or elastic changes in materials or products, or a temperature increase may be converted into force, which in turn produces irreversible plastic changes in the shape of materials or products.

These materials and products can be divided into different groups depending on their ability to change their properties or have them changed by outside influences.

SHAPE-CHANGING NON- AND SEMI-SMART MATERIALS

Depending on the material, its thickness and final required shape, tools and machinery are normally required to deform solid metal sheets in three dimensions. Conventional metal can only be deformed using relatively little force if the metal is woven or stamped in advance into a more reshapable structure. Expanded metal is one such material, but it can only be deformed in three dimensions to a limited extent.

A relatively new perforated sheet made from aluminium behaves in a different way. It can be easily worked by hand, stretched or upset. In this example, a pattern of Y-shaped holes (in the Formetal product) allows the material to be easily deformed in three dimensions.

Heat-shrinkable materials in the form of film or sleeves are among those materials and products that change their shape plastically and irreversibly in response to increased temperature. Examples of their use include the manufacture of packaging and cable sleeves to protect items from moisture and hold them in position.

Under certain circumstances it is worthwhile using materials or products that partially or fully dissolve after a preset period of time or at the end of their useful lives. They could be temporary materials used for example during the manufacture of a component and then decomposed later by some external influence; or components in their own right that decompose themselves after they are no longer in use. Although these processes are not reversible, they promise a variety of interesting applications in architecture.

Lamp in the shape of a bear, yellow plastic body with a shaped Formetal perforated sheet. | *Audi-Kreationsei* in a pavilion at the Volkswagen "Car City" in Dresden, skin made from Formetal. | Sections of heat-shrinkable sleeve before and after heat treatment.

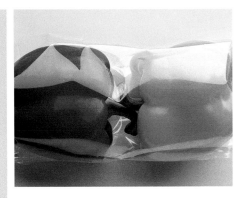

Materials and products with the property of decomposition have been mainly developed with the aim of waste prevention. So-called biodegradable materials are developed and brought on to the market for a range of applications, e.g. for use as package fillings, packaging, fast-food cutlery etc. For such uses, materials based on mineral oils are processed into polyesters; vegetable-based materials into starches, polylactic acids, cellulose acetates; and the mixtures manufactured from them into starch blends among others. These products are completely broken down by bacterial or fungal attack.

In contrast to the above there are also materials that decompose on contact with water alone. The products made from them include cold, warm and hot water degradable films, which can be further processed into bags and cold water degradable fleeces. Polyvinyl alcohol (PVAL)-based films were introduced as detergent packaging in 1961. Today they are also used as temporary stiffening inserts for textiles that are to be stitched e.g. with filigree patterns, which in turn are later removed by washing. Or they are used in product areas where their contents are intended to be released by contact with water. In architecture they could be used as temporary protective packaging for small moisture-insensitive construction elements. The protective packaging is designed to decompose in contact with hot water after transport to site, but not with rainwater.

In addition to the above, there is a further form of disintegration and decomposition that has not been sufficiently investigated and developed at the moment and could have a role in the future: the use of materials fitted with a special switch to trigger the decomposition process after a period of time and/or in response to a particular stimulus. It would be possible to use gene technology here to modify conventional materials in an appropriate way.

COLOUR- AND OPTICALLY CHANGING NON- AND SEMI-SMART MATERIALS

Surfaces that change colour depending on the angle of view are not smart materials but are of interest in the field of architecture. These types of material include dyes with special-effect pigments.

Dichroitic and holographic optical materials and products made from them are further examples. Dichroitic materials and products have the ability to appear to change colour when viewed from different angles. This effect is caused by the light falling upon them being decomposed into reflected and transmitted radiation spectra. Dichroitic filters applied to glazing are of particular interest to architects. These filters consist of systems of perhaps 10 to 20 alternately low- and high-refracting layers of various thicknesses. The typical thickness of these layers is between 45 nm and 110 nm. The layers are applied using the Sol-Gel process. Therefore they are suitable for application on surfaces curved in two dimensions, but on surfaces and bodies with three-dimensional curvature it is not usually possible to achieve an adequately even coating.

Biophan film made from polylactic acid (PLA). I Sushi catering dishes made from Mater-Bi (starch material).

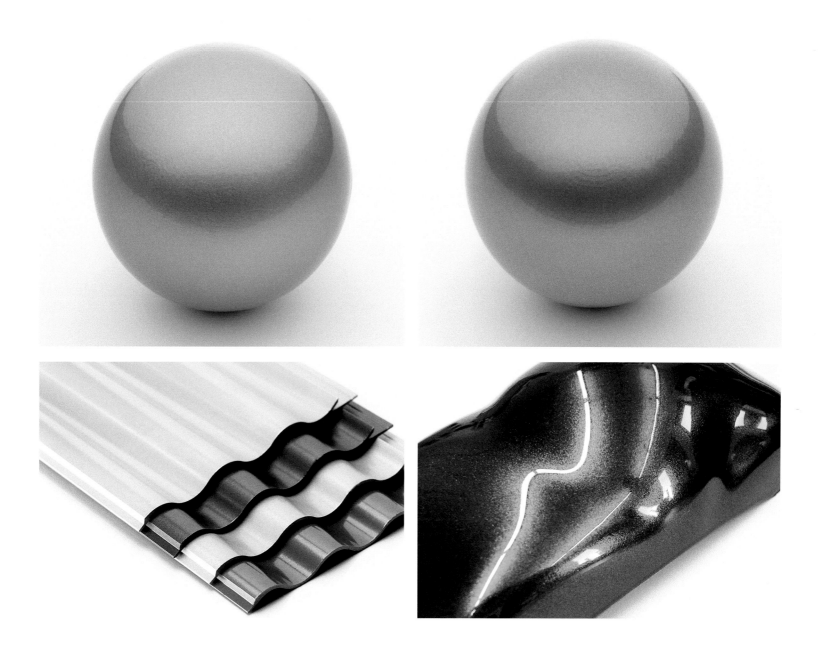

Effect paint on bodies with smooth, spherical surfaces (Colorstream: Lapis Sunlight, Tropic Sunrise). | Corrugated sheet with effect paint (Colorstream). | Effect paint on an object with an irregularly shaped surface (Xirallic Cosmic Turquoise).

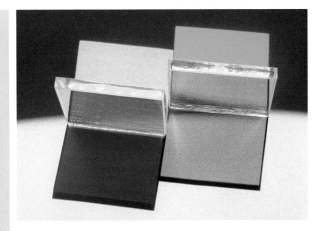

Dichroitic filters on glass, applied in a right angle to a white paper substrate to make the reflection and transmission colours visible. | Dichroitic filters on glass tube sections. | Details of HoloPro.

Lobby of the Copenhagen Opera House with three chandeliers. The glass surfaces are coated with dichroitic filters. | View from below into one of the three glass bodies.

Facade with holographic glazing: *Augenfeuer*,
Michael Bleyenberg. | *opposite: Augenfeuer.*

Berlin-domiciled artist Olafur Eliasson, working with A. P. Møller and Chastine McKinney of the Møller Foundation, designed a 2.9 m diameter, spherical chandelier made from 1480 triangles of laminated safety glass fitted with dichroitic filters for the Copenhagen Opera House. Three of these objects were installed in 2004 in the opera house lobby.

Originally used to direct light through optics, holographic optical elements (HOE) were further developed at the Institute of Light and Construction Technology at the Cologne University of Applied Sciences in Germany as a potentially new means of directing light through glass facades. The results of this research provided the basis for a new company that specialises in the manufacture of transparent projection surfaces capable of showing video projections with daylight brightness. An important part of HoloPro and HoloSign, the latter being a variant derived from HoloPro which is used to display permanent graphics, is a holographic film embedded between two transparent substrates (e.g. glass or PMMA) on which a multitude of these HOEs are applied close to one another using a special process.

In addition to some purely artistic applications, HoloSign has already found uses in the field of architecture. Working with the Institute of Light and Construction Technology, the Cologne-based artist Michael Bleyenberg used this product in 2000 in the facade of a new extension to the German Research Foundation (DFG) in Bonn. The 5 m x 13 m work *Augenfeuer* contains graphical elements in various colours, their optical presence and colour depending on the angle of view and solar position. Diffraction and interference of the light falling on the holographic layer create the five colours red, orange, yellow, green and blue.

Of further interest in this context are new transparent construction elements that consist of a multitude of passive illuminating plastic fibre optic cables interlinked on an irregular basis. In this way the places where light falls and is emitted are not positioned directly over one another, which means that light and shadow appear in other than the expected places. These elements could be integrated in the form of blocks or panels into facades.

opposite: Show room (X-Box) with fibre optic cable panels (SensiTile) integrated into the tables. | Close-up photograph. | Various transparent and coloured fibre optic cable panels (SensiTile).

VISCOSITY-CHANGING SEMI-SMART AND SMART MATERIALS

These smart materials include materials and products that are able to reversibly change their flow properties in response to one or more stimuli, for example the influence of mechanical energy (e.g. tension) or the application of an electrical and/or magnetic field.

Thixotropic fluids (TF), electrorheologic fluids (ERF) and magnetorheologic fluids (MRF) are of interest for architectural applications, but so far there have been few implementations. TFs for example are mixtures of water and sand that liquefy when subject to abrupt movements. Unlike ERFs and MRFs no conversion of the introduced energy takes place, hence they are considered as semi-smart materials.

ERFs are stable suspensions of minute, electrically polarisable particles in a non-electrically polarisable carrier liquid. By applying an electrical field, their viscosities can be infinitely variably and reversibly changed in milliseconds. The suspensions generally consist of mineral or silicon oils.

In contrast, MRFs are stable suspensions of minute, magnetically polarisable particles in a non-magnetic carrier liquid. By applying a magnetic field, their viscosities as well can be infinitely variably and reversibly changed in milliseconds. In addition to rheological behaviour, the electrical, thermal, acoustic and optical properties of the suspensions change at the same time. They consist of mineral or synthetic oils, water or glycol, in which are suspended up to 20% to 40% of e.g. iron particles with a diameter of 3 to 10 microns.

In both fluids the particles are randomly distributed in the carrier liquid. When subjected to an electrical or magnetic field, they form long chains capable of carrying mechanical loads to a greater or lesser extent, which can be then deformed or broken by outside influences.

"Smart Damping Strategies for Seismic Protection of Urban Structures", a project headed by B. F. Spencer, Professor at the University of Illinois, and managed by the US-American-Japanese Urban Earthquake Disaster Mitigation Research Initiative, concentrated on the development of shock absorbers incorporating MRFs for use in non-military buildings. The result was a large-scale seismic shock damper, two examples of which were manufactured for installation in the new Nihon-Kagaku-Miraikan building in Tokyo Bay, Japan. The dampers were incorporated as an integral component of the main load-bearing structure by a lever mechanism below a V-shaped bracing between the 3rd and 5th floors. Both dampers are only a short height off the floor and are therefore convenient to inspect, easy to maintain and, if necessary, replace.

In the event of horizontal movement of the building induced by seismic movements of the Earth's surface, the two bracings displace the pistons in the dampers by means of the lever mechanisms to provide the desired shock damping effect in the adaptive system.

Illustration of the electrorheologic effect (comparable to the magnetorheologic effect). | Technology by Lord: typical MRF. | Various products incorporating MRFs. | Small shock absorber incorporating MRF. | Technology by Fludicon: Prototypes of actuating and positioning drives incorporating ERFs.

Large-scale seismic shock damper: V-shaped bracing forming part
of the main load-bearing structure with the lever mechanism.

Luminating textile with a pattern in various colours. l
Luminating textile as a blind.

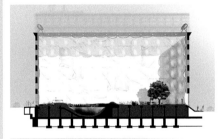

Solare Schiller-Zitat-Tafel (Solar Schiller quotation board) on the city wall in Marbach am Neckar, Germany, consisting of nine modules 1.20 m x 1.20 m | Technology by Sharp: Katsuragi plant at night | Idea for a membrane that uses nanofiltration to keep a dwelling pollutant-free: *You've Gotta Have Faith*, Daniel Pelosi, 2005.

LIGHT-EMITTING NON- AND SEMI-SMART MATERIALS

Not all light-emitting materials and products can be classed as smart materials. An important criterion for this is that most of the available energy, e.g. in the form of light or electric current, is used in the emission of cold light. Consequently, materials and products that emit a large amount of heat in addition to light are not classed as smart materials.

A relatively new development in this context are luminating textiles in which projectors are incorporated to illuminate light-conducting fibres. The light sources in the projectors are sodium vapour lamps, which develop a lot of heat.

MATTER-EMITTING NON- AND SEMI-SMART MATERIALS

In addition to taking in matter (see matter-exchanging smart materials, pp. 174 ff.), for example by the adsorption or absorption of substances (components), which can be used for room air improvement among other functions, the release of matter by certain substances may also be desirable. Apart from the normal and permanent exchange of substances between room or furnishing surfaces and the room air, certain other materials that give off scents when touched, heated or due to other influences are also of interest. These materials include paints, often in the form of inks, containing microencapsulated scents. They can be applied by screen printing on paper, cardboard and other suitable surfaces. As they become exhausted over a period of time, they cannot be considered to be smart materials.

ELECTRICITY-GENERATING MATERIALS AND PRODUCTS

Silicon-based solar cells are the main type of electricity-generating materials and products that have found practical applications, some in the field of architecture. Thin-film and organic solar cells are relatively new developments. In addition to these, dye solar cells (DSC), thermoelectric generators (TEG) and systems based on piezoelectric materials are available for various uses and are dealt with in the main part of this book.

Hybrid poly-smart systems that consist of solar cells with integrated light-emitting diodes (LED) are also of interest here. They generate electricity by day, used by the system to provide light during the night.

Tiles partially coated with hydrophobic nanometre-scale particles to create graphics and characters which appear in reaction to moisture: *Hydrophobic Nanotiles*, Peter Yeadon, 2004. | Polymorphic smart material consisting of nanometre-scale rod elements: *nBot Nanorobotic Environments*, Peter Yeadon, 2005. | Simulation of a collapsed *Utility Fog* dome above the lower part of Manhattan Island. | Slabs of debris and pieces of the *Utility Fog* as potential backdrop for an underground theatre group: *Dystopic Scenarios*, Jaithan Kochar, 2005.

HYBRID MATERIALS AND PRODUCTS

By combining individual materials to form hybrid materials and products, high-power mutually enhancing systems, like the solar cell-LED system described above, can be created. Some insulation systems that fully achieve their extraordinary properties only when combined with other materials are of interest for architectural applications. These product types include vacuum insulation panels (VIP), which are already on the market, and the yet-to-be-introduced switchable thermal insulation (STI) developed at the Bavarian Applied Energy Research Centre (ZAE Bayern) in Germany. The latter product is based on VIP technology with the addition and integration of a metal hydride, which changes the thermal conductivity of the panels in response to the taking-up and release of small quantities of hydrogen.

NANOMATERIALS AND NANOPRODUCTS

The development and manufacture of materials and products from nanometre-scale substances has opened up possibilities for new and innovative functions. These innovations include layers of nanoparticles which can make glazing especially water-repellent or spectrum-selective, or paints and plastics extremely scratch-resistant. Glazing can incorporate suitably thin dichroitic filter layers. Nanoparticles can also be used in gypsum wallboard to improve room air quality. Examples of nanoparticles used here are titanium dioxide (TiO_2) and zeolite (see mineral ad-/absorbents (MAd, MAb), pp. 175 ff.). In a similar context, membranes with nanometre-scale pores are currently being developed to be used as part of facades with the ability to clean polluted city air.

Although the possibilities of these nanometre-scale substances seem unlimited, their use has not been totally without opposition. There are concerns about their potentially hazardous effects on health, which have been raised by research into extremely small particles.

Another development are the so-called polymorphic smart materials based on programmable mechanical units. Their minute size of only a few nanometres, their ability to change their geometry and reconfigure their links with one another means they can take up a wide range of physical and optical states. One of these polymorphs is the visionary smart material *Utility Fog*, conceived by J. Storrs Hall at the beginning of 1990s. The *Utility Fog* consists of a multitude of round nanometric robots, so-called nanobots, with connecting arms and described by Storrs Hall as foglets. By giving them telescopic arms that can articulate and connect in different ways, the foglets would be able, according to the scientist, to simultaneously create gaseous, liquid and solid materials with various reversible properties.

Among the organisations currently working on the realisation of this technology is the Institute for Molecular Manufacturing in Palo Alto, USA, as is demonstrated by the work of Jaithan Kochar. Kochar, who, like Daniel Pelosi, is a student at the Future Studio of the Rhode Island School of Design, Providence, USA, worked under Prof. Peter Yeadon and looked into the possible dangers Utility Fog might present. He envisioned a scenario in which a giant Utility Fog dome protecting Lower Manhattan from negative atmospheric effects fails and collapses.

smart materials

MATERIALS, PRODUCTS, PROJECTS

shape-changing smart materials

Shape-changing smart materials include materials and products that are able to reversibly change their shape and/or dimensions in response to one or more stimuli through external influences, the effect of light, temperature, pressure, an electric or magnetic field, or a chemical stimulus. Among these, there are materials and products that are able to change their shape without changing their dimensions, and other materials and products that retain their shape but change their dimensions. Some are also able to change both parameters at the same time.

The inherent properties of these smart materials depend on the different principles behind their deformation. Depending on the distribution and arrangement of the sensitive components and a basic geometric shape, changes may take place in all dimensions to equal or unequal extents. Smart materials that have a single active sensitive component generally expand or contract evenly; the same applies to smart materials that are composed of a passive component, e.g. the carrier material (matrix), and an evenly distributed active component. If on the other hand the passive and active components are unevenly distributed, for example if two differently sensitive components are arranged in layers one on top of the other, then the material or product will deform on one side only.

The currently available shape-changing materials can be differentiated according to their triggering stimuli as follows

PHOTOSTRICTIVE SMART MATERIALS
Excited by the effect of light (electromagnetic energy).
THERMOSTRICTIVE SMART MATERIALS
Excited by the effect of temperature (thermal energy).
PIEZOELECTRIC SMART MATERIALS
Excited by the effect of pressure or tension (mechanical energy).
ELECTROACTIVE SMART MATERIALS
Excited by the effect of an electric field (electrical energy).
MAGNETOSTRICTIVE SMART MATERIALS
Excited by the effect of a magnetic field (magnetic energy).
CHEMOSTRICTIVE SMART MATERIALS
Excited by the effect of a chemical environment (chemical energy).

Thermostrictive, piezoelectric, electroactive and chemostrictive smart materials are those that are currently of the greatest interest in the field of architecture, due to their availability, predicted long-term stability and other factors. Assuming successful further development and market placement, the near future could see other smart materials gaining in importance, including photostrictive and magnetostrictive ones. Piezoelectric smart materials are discussed elsewhere (see piezoelectric ceramics/polymers (PEC, PEP), pp. 154 ff.)

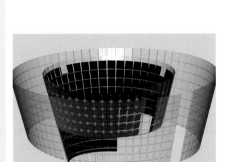

Documentation Centre at the Former Concentration Camp, Hinzert: inner ring structure with kinetic cladding transmitting variable amounts of light, outer ring structure made from transparent thermal insulation | *BalnaeNY:* variously deformed sauna walls with EAP, projecting into the street space

**THERMOSTRICTIVE SMART MATERIALS >
MATERIALS, PRODUCTS, PROJECTS**

Thermostrictive smart materials have inherent properties that enable them to react to ambient temperature changes by reversibly changing their shape and/or dimensions. The temperature changes may have a passive effect by which the material continually adjusts its internal thermal state to its natural surroundings through its surface. They may also have an active effect, for example by heating or cooling. Active heating may be either direct heating by the application of an electrical field or indirect heating by heat conduction or radiation.

In the field of architecture the following thermostrictive smart materials among others are currently of interest:

THERMAL EXPANSION MATERIALS (TEM)/EXPANSION MATERIALS (EM)

THERMOBIMETALS (TB)

SHAPE MEMORY ALLOYS (SMA)

Other thermostrictive smart materials are:

THERMOBICOMPOSITE MATERIALS

SHAPE MEMORY POLYMERS (SMP)

SHAPE MEMORY FOAMS

SHAPE MEMORY CERAMICS

BIOLOGICAL SYSTEMS WITH SHAPE MEMORY EFFECT

thermal expansion materials (TEM) / expansion materials (EM) › materials

Thermal expansion materials (TEM) are materials with a coefficient of thermal expansion that is markedly positive or negative or one that is almost zero. They are referred to accordingly as positive thermal expansion materials (PTEM), negative thermal expansion materials (NTEM) and zero thermal expansion materials (ZTEM).

Expansion materials (EM) classed as PTEMs are suitable for use as pressure-controlling media, e.g. to operate piston-controlled working elements (linear actuators). Depending on the material, the phase change may have different effects. Some materials undergo a continuous change in volume in response to a continuous change in temperature, whilst other EMs undergo a discontinuous, sudden (i.e. at particular points) volume change in response to a continuous temperature change. Certain EMs can also be used as latent heat storage. They are called phase change materials (PCM) (see phase change materials (PCM), pp. 165 ff.).

Thermometers were one of the first applications of gaseous and liquid EMs. Galileo Galilei is credited with inventing the first temperature gauge (1592-98), which used an air-filled glass bulb, the extended open end of which was immersed in coloured water. The enclosed air expands depending on the prevalent air temperature and determines the height of the column of water. By the middle of the 17th century, liquid media such as ethyl alcohol and mercury were also in use. The sprinkler system invented by American Henry S. Parmalee in 1874 first used fusible links, which melted under thermal load and triggered the release of the extinguishing water. Glass ampoules containing thermally sensitive EMs were later developed for this role. For a period of several decades EMs have been used as pressure media in working elements.

Materials and components generally used include among others:

ALKANES (EXPANSION WAX)
n-alkanes, paraffin oils, paraffin waxes.

ALCOHOLS
Glycerine.

OTHERS
Tetrachloroethylene, 1.3-dioxolane.

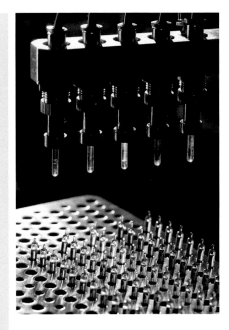

Sprinkler ampoules during manufacture | Sprinkler ampoules filled with coloured thermally sensitive EMs. | Sprinkler heads with ampoules.

The following EMs are among those of interest in architecture:

N-ALKANES C10 TO C18
Colourless hydrocarbons, liquid at +20°C, are used for EM working elements at low temperatures.
➕ Market presence, can be made in large quantities, many years of practical use, can be used in low temperatures (−16°C to +40°C), insensitive to mechanical vibrations, maintenance-free, long replacement life.
➖ Major leakages may be hazardous to ground water, may convert or break down into water and carbon dioxide on contact with air or oxygen, inflammable gases may form in contact with air.

PARAFFIN OIL, PARAFFIN WAX
Depending on the state, colourless to whitish-yellow hydrocarbons, liquid to solid at +20°C; used for EM working elements with continuous linear or discontinuous sudden (i.e. at particular points) expansion behaviour.
➕ Can be used in medium to high temperatures (0°C to +180°C), paraffin waxes solid at +20°C cannot liquidise in the presence of air. Otherwise as above.
➖ As above.

thermal expansion materials (TEM) / expansion materials (EM) › products

Since their first use in a thermometer, expansion materials (EM) have been developed into a wide range of products and brought on to the market for a wide range of applications. Comparatively sluggish reaction times have resulted in the EM working elements being increasingly replaced in some sectors with quicker and more precisely reactive working elements, for example with electrorheologic fluids (see p. 38). New, previously unexploited possibilities are appearing for some applications, including some in the field of architecture.

EMs in glass ampoules are still used today as components in sprinkler systems. Another application is as a working medium in EM working elements, e.g. for operating valves, controlling gases and liquids. The main areas of use are in automobile construction and building technical services, e.g. in heating thermostats. EM working elements are sometimes used as actuator or positioner drives in greenhouses and building facades in energy-autonomous, decentralised room ventilation systems.

EM working elements:

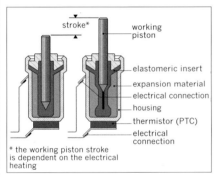

stroke*

working piston

elastomeric insert
expansion material
electrical connection
housing
thermistor (PTC)
electrical connection

* the working piston stroke is dependent on the electrical heating

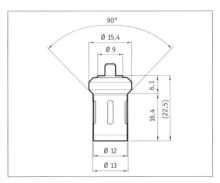

90°
Ø 15,4
Ø 9
6,1
16,4
(22,5)
Ø 12
Ø 13

EM working elements with elastomeric insert and PTC thermistor. | Operation of EM working elements | Typical dimensions.

ACTUATOR OR POSITIONER DRIVES (LINEAR ACTUATORS)

These devices generally consist of a pressure-resistant vessel filled with an EM that expands on being heated to displace an actuating piston outwards. The piston moves back either under the action of a return spring or an external force. Architectural applications may require longer travel distances and therefore greater actuating forces than drives in the automobile industry or building technical services. They have been developed and manufactured in various sizes and with different container materials for a variety of functions. Their rather sluggish reaction times are normally adequate for many applications.

Various assemblies with different actuator or positioner drives can be constructed by fitting different add-on pieces such as connecting plates and/or lever mechanisms, or by the incorporation into passive components of varying complexity.

➕ Create continuous, almost linear, or discontinuous, sudden movements depending on the EM used, relatively long actuator path (here the lifting range for positioning components) compared with e.g. piezoelectrically operated actuator and positioner drives, relatively compact construction, no electricity supply required, not noisy, relatively inexpensive.

➖ Relatively sluggish reaction times compared with e.g. piezoelectrically operated actuator and positioner drives, can be damaged if the thermal load significantly exceeds the operating range.

ACTUATOR AND POSITIONER DRIVES (LINEAR ACTUATORS) WITH PTC THERMISTORS (POSITIVE TEMPERATURE COEFFICIENT THERMISTORS)

EM working elements fitted for direct heating: they have an electrically heated positive temperature coefficient (PTC) thermistor manufactured from doped polycrystalline ceramic with barium titanate (see piezoelectric ceramics/polymers (PEC, PEP), pp. 154 ff.). Otherwise as above.

➕ No heat-conducting medium required, which leads to quicker response times and possible reduced size, can be thermally or electrically controlled, can operate at different electrical voltages (low voltage), relatively better thermal overload resistance compared with purely thermally controlled actuator and positioner drives.

➖ Electricity supply required for PTC thermistors.

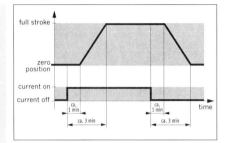

Assemblies of working elements with EM:

ACTUATOR AND POSITIONER DRIVES WITH LEVER MECHANISM
EM working elements fitted with a lever mechanism to amplify the travel distance and an integrated reset spring to return the actuator piston. Otherwise as for actuator and positioner drives.
+ Relatively long travel paths, quicker response times compared with conventional actuator and positioner drives, special connections can be fitted. Otherwise as for actuator and positioner drives.
– Can be damaged if the thermal expansion is constrained. Otherwise as for actuator and positioner drives.

General recommendations: To guarantee the proper functioning of the EM working elements over a long period, the thermal load must not significantly exceed the specified operating range (normally 12 K to15 K) as the excessive expansion of the EM could destroy the elements. Depending on the installed heat-transmitting medium or the surrounding environment, the pressure-resistant vessel can be made of brass, aluminium, stainless steel or copper. Several EM working elements can be fitted in parallel and/or series to increase the capacity when used as an actuator or positioner drive.

thermal expansion materials (тєm) / expansion materials (єm) › projects

Other than the already mentioned use in sprinkler ampoules, expansion materials (EM) have also been used for decades as heating thermostat components. For some years now, automatic ventilation units have been available that open and close at certain temperatures to allow enclosed rooms to be ventilated. They usually work by raising or lowering some part of the roof or may be designed as special ventilation elements in building facades.

Although the idea might seem obvious, there has been no use of EMs in conjunction with automatically guided systems to form adaptive, mechanical, light-directing or shade-creating systems.

Two projects where thermo-, or light- and thermosensitive EM working elements are used as actuator or positioner drives to manipulate architectonic structures are outlined below.

Products currently used in architecture include:

RAW OR END PRODUCTS:

WORKING ELEMENTS with EMs Assemblies with working elements with EMs

self-constructing tower

Monosmart material | Monosmart application
Shape-changing smart materials:
EM WORKING ELEMENTS (LINEAR ACTUATORS)
Temperature-dependent kinetic structure

Peter Linnett, **Toby Blunt**, Great Britain
Kinetic room installation for the Bath Festival |
Bath, Great Britain (1996)

Although it remains to be built, the kinetic three-dimensional installation called *Self-Constructing Tower*, designed in Scotland in 1996 by Scottish artist Peter Linnett together with architect Toby Blunt for the Bath Festival, shows how EM working elements, described by the designers as thermohydraulic actuators, could be used in shape-varying room-forming structures.

The installation was planned for a site on the bank of the River Avon: placed on the wall coping above an arched window of a derelict warehouse, the three-part moving structure, insect-like in the proportions of its body, was designed to react automatically to its immediate environmental surroundings and unfold or close up like a flower, depending on wind, sun, air temperature and water level.

The EM working elements were designed to operate in three axes arranged around a central node. Each of the two projecting, carbon-fibre, 6 m long aerofoil elements would change its position by means of temperature-reactive actuating processes: on mild days the structure would unfold up to a height of 15 m, whilst during cold nights or bad weather it would retract into the window arch.

For safety reasons it was necessary to specify a clear area of at least 20 m around the structure. In place of this dynamically reactive tower the visitors to the Bath Festival were presented with a simple structure without EM working elements.

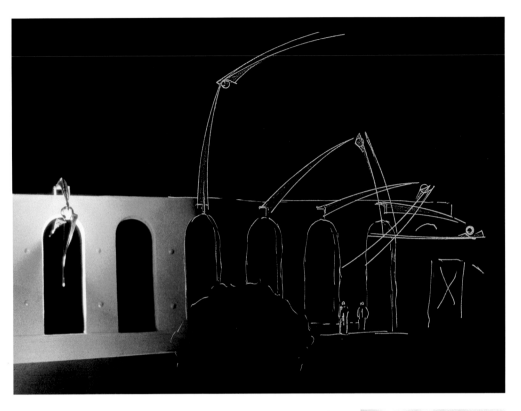

Self-Constructing Tower: illustration. | Sketch showing possible positions. | Model in bad and in changeable weather. | *opposite:* Time-stroke graph.

Documentation centre at the former concentration camp, Hinzert

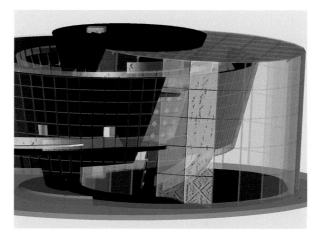

Monosmart materials | Polysmart application
Shape-changing smart materials:
EM WORKING ELEMENTS (LINEAR ACTUATORS) WITH
PTC THERMISTORS
Electricity-generating smart materials:
THIN FILM SOLAR CELLS
Light- and temperature-dependent kinetic structure

Axel Ritter, Germany
Kinetic facade for a documentation and meeting centre on the former
SS Special Camp/Concentration Camp at Hinzert | Germany (2004)

An architectural competition for the planned construction of a new documentation and meeting centre on the site of the former concentration camp at Hinzert, Germany, was held in 2004.

The circular shape of the existing 1986 memorial and parts of the route the visitors take, clearly sets them apart from the right-angled geometry of the former concentration camp buildings. The architect adopted this rounded shape as the main design and organisation principle of his dynamic reinterpretation. His design creates a structure based on four rings, embracing one another, some conically tapering and cut at an angle. The two outer rings contain the library and conference room whilst another takes the form of a three-storey glass cylinder inserted into the rings to create two exhibition areas with quite different atmospheres. The partly open space included between them acts as a foyer.

The walls forming the foyer consist of a circular, frameless glass facade construction with an outside cladding which is kinetic, transmits variable amounts of light and has diagonally divided panels that pivot to open to varying degrees. Thin film solar cells are used with PTC thermistors in the EM working elements to allow the cladding automatically to control the amount of light inside the building. To limit thermal effects and to ensure that light alone is the controlling stimulus, the EM working element housings are enclosed individually in thermal insulation. At the same time the individual corners of the dynamic facade slabs, moving outwards over a large area in response to light, are suggestive of "barbed wire" and "threat." Solar cells and collectors on the roofs complete the energy concept.

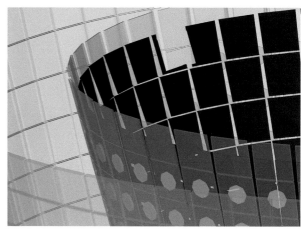

Documentation Centre at the Former Concentration Camp, Hinzert: perspective side view. | Perspective overhead view/plan. | Detail of kinetic facade, partially open.

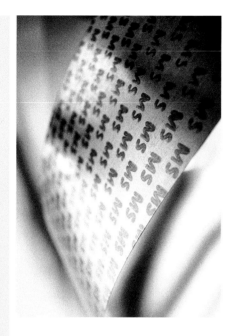

thermobimetals (TB) › materials

Thermobimetals (TB) are laminated composite materials and consist of at least two components, usually bands or strips, made from metals with different thermal expansion coefficients, which are permanently bonded to one another, for example by plating. The component with the lower coefficient of thermal expansion is called passive, the one with the higher coefficient active. Depending on the way the temperature changes over time, the components used and their geometries, the composite takes up a curved shape and can be used for various applications and purposes.

The terms used in Europe to describe TBs refer to the composition of the active component alloy, whilst the Americans refer to that of the passive component.

TBs are relatively old smart materials and have been around since the beginning of the industrial revolution. Today they are mainly used in measurement and control systems, e.g. as thermostats, and with electrical control as components in mechatronic systems.

As passive components they include:

ALLOYS
Iron-nickel (Invar), nickel-cobalt-iron (Superinvar)

As active components they include:

ALLOYS
Iron-nickel-manganese, manganese-nickel-copper, iron-nickel-manganese and copper

TBs can be made corrosion-resistant by plating with chrome and copper, and their electrical conductivity improved for active heat gain by incorporating a layer of copper between the two components.

Components for the manufacture of TBs should possess good platability, hot and cold ductility, a high melting point, a high modulus of elasticity (Young's modulus), high strength and predictable behaviour. Furthermore, a certain range of divergent behaviour regarding the melting point, modulus of elasticity and strength of components should not be exceeded. Specific dimensional relationships are to be maintained.

TB strips with nickel-cobalt-iron (Superinvar) as the passive component and manganese-nickel-copper as the active one.

Simple strips with different shapes and component combinations. | Spirals with corrosion-resistant chromium coating. | Helix.

The following component combinations are among those of interest in architecture:

NICKEL-COBALT-IRON (SUPERINVAR) WITH MANGANESE-NICKEL-COPPER
+ Market presence, can be made in large quantities, many years of practical use, excellent thermal sensitivity, wide range of applications, can be made resistant to rusting and other corrosion effects by additional rolled-on layers, can also be made in small quantities.
– Relatively expensive compared with component combinations without e.g. Superinvar as the active component

NICKEL-COBALT-IRON (SUPERINVAR) WITH IRON-NICKEL-MANGANESE AND COPPER
+ Suitable for applications using direct electrical heating. Otherwise as above.
– As above.

thermobimetals (TB) › products

Many years of market presence and continuous further development, particularly in relation to the manufacture of complicated shapes and assemblies, have meant that today complex products made of thermobimetals (TB) are manufactured, mostly for specific applications. TBs may be produced as raw, intermediate and end products depending on the number of process steps and the intended purpose.

TBs currently available as raw material products include:

TB bands:

SIMPLE STRIPS, U-PROFILE CURVED STRIPS
They can be installed as clamped at one or both ends.
+ Can be used as actuator or positioner drives to create continuous, almost linear movement, medium movement capacity, can be used in various ways as a variable force spring, relatively inexpensive compared with other control elements. Otherwise as for alloys above.
– Relatively sluggish reaction times compared with other actuator or positioner drives. Otherwise as for alloys above.

REVERSE STRIPS
They can also be installed as clamped on one or both ends.
+ Can achieve relatively longer straight-line movements compared to e.g. TB creep-action discs. Otherwise as above.
– As above.

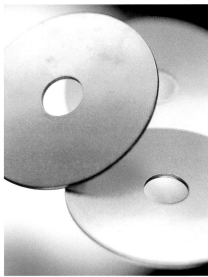

Snap-action discs. | Creep-action discs with
corrosion-resistant copper coating.

SPIRALS, HELICES

They can be installed as clamped at one end.

+ Spirals, helices
They can be installed as clamped at one end.

− As above.

Parts made from TBs:

CREEP-ACTION DISCS

They can be used singly, or in series to amplify the effect, held in position at their centres
or in a sleeve.

+ Can be used as actuator or positioner drives for creating continuous linear movements.
Otherwise as above.

− As above.

SNAP-ACTION DISCS

They can be installed in the same way as creep-action discs.

+ Can be used as actuator or positioner drives for creating continuous and sudden (at
preset points) linear movements. Otherwise as above.

− As above.

STAMPED PARTS

They can be clamped in various ways depending on shape and function.

+ Complex two-dimensional shapes possible, three-dimensional shapes can be produced by
folding. Otherwise as above.

− As above.

ASSEMBLIES WITH TBs: BANDS, PARTS MADE FROM TBs AND OTHER MATERIALS

Can be installed in the same way as stamped parts.

+ Special connections and complex three-dimensional shapes can be fabricated. Otherwise
as above.

− Relatively expensive compared with bands and parts made from TBs. Otherwise as above.

General recommendations for use: to ensure a long replacement life the products should not be loaded up to their limits. The application of an additional rolled-on layer of stainless steel should be applied as a means of preventing rust and other corrosion phenomena, depending on the expected environment and the component combinations. Several TB elements can be arranged in series and/or in parallel to increase the performance capacity especially when used as actuating elements.

thermobimetals (TB) › projects

As an extension of their usual scope of applications, thermobimetals (TB) can also be used directly in architecture. This applies in particular to their use for actuation, control and regulation, and as spring and compensation elements. So far, however, few applications in architecture have become known or documented. Automatically opening and closing ventilation flaps have been developed and installed in greenhouses and for use as self-closing fire protection flaps. Currently, a self-actuated clamping mechanism based on TBs for use with less expensive fire protection doors is being developed. The clamping mechanism prevents the door from warping and releasing combustion gases into other parts of the building. It should also be possible to develop self-actuating air intake and exhaust openings for facades, which would react to outside temperatures, but so far no practical solutions have been implemented.

A possible architectural application of a polyreactive mechanomembrane, which could be further developed for large-scale use as part of a weather-sensitive building envelope, is outlined below.

Products currently in use in architecture or likely to become relevant in the future include:

RAW OR END PRODUCTS:

TB BANDS

PARTS MADE from TBs
ASSEMBLIES with TBs

INTERMEDIATE OR END PRODUCTS:

ACTUATOR or POSITIONER DRIVES MADE from or incorporating TBs

CONTROL and REGULATING ELEMENTS made from or incorporating TBs

SPRING ELEMENTS with variable/varying spring force made from or incorporating TBs

COMPENSATING ELEMENTS made from or incorporating TBs

polyreactive mechanomembrane

Monosmart materials | Polysmart application
Shape-changing smart materials:
COLOUR INDICATOR BALLS WITH THERMOBIMETAL AND
HYGROBICOMPOSITE SPIRAL SPRINGS (TB, HB)
Weather-dependent kinetic colour-changing structure

Axel Ritter, Germany
Weather-sensitive kinetic building envelope | Germany (1997)

The development of the polyreactive mechanomembrane, a bionically in-spired membrane with weather-sensitive components, demonstrates how, in future constructions, building envelopes can be made to resemble highly complex mechanical systems.

In his design approach based on a technical implementation of the model of the human skin as a building envelope, the author has analysed its anat-omy and characteristics, especially its ability to change. The following abili-ties, in particular, of the human skin to react to outside influences looked promising for a building envelope and appeared capable of being adapted and technically implemented, given appropriately reactive structures and the use of smart materials: the ability to reversibly deform in three dimen-sions by expanding in response to direct mechanical load or by active con-traction of the skin muscles, the ability to change colour by going brown or reddening and the ability to regulate temperature by actively exuding liquid and exploiting the resulting cooling effect of evaporation. Like the reactions of the skin and the connected nerve systems, the reactions of the technical membrane would be determined by the weather.

The membrane was to have an adequate elastic matrix to resist mechanical loads, be able to change colour in response to changes of temperature and humidity in the surrounding air, and regulate its own temperature like its natural role model by taking up or exuding the required moisture through the membrane in the form of rainwater.

The construction of a technology demonstrator was to prove the feasibility of such a membrane and its suitability for daily use. The effectiveness of the mechanical processes involved is ensured by acrylic glass balls of various diameters, which accommodate all the different functional units and other autonomic reactive components. For this, modular units with six balls have been developed, which, in combination with three variously arranged pro-jecting support arms, form three-dimensional structures and are flexibly joined to one another by elastic bands.

Polyreactive mechanomembrane: building elements. | *opposite:* Assembly with EM working element: actuator and positioner drive with lever mechanism.

Each module consists of two balls with openings to take in water, which are kept apart by a tension spring. They contain a strip filter to separate rain water; on the bottom two silicone hoses are connected, the rearmost one of which flows into a larger water storage ball carried on a moving support arm. A transpirator ring of water-absorbing porous ceramic material is mounted on a base plate around each one, from which a further laterally connected support arm extends and carries a colour indicator ball. One half of the 40 colour indicator balls is fitted with TB spiral springs and a composite material that is sensitive to air humidity. The other balls are fitted with TB spiral springs only, which displace the colour and colour filter surfaces in response to temperature and air humidity and thus indicate the energy and constituent states of the surrounding air.

A TB spiral spring attached to the underside of each base plate reacts to temperature by bringing a connected wick, which ends in a water storage ball, into contact with the transpirator ring and thus initiates the evaporation process.

On the outside, to protect the mechanical structure and enclose the building, the membrane has a flexible, fine-meshed textile covering membrane with a narrow opening in its rainwater inlets near each water receiving ball. The outside structure is changed in response to the weight of the water storage balls by means of pairs of V-shaped spring steel hairs that are attached on their inside to the water storage balls and on their outside project through the textile membrane. The hairs are able to stand out or contract depending on the energy state, thus imitating the changing surface structures of the human skin.

Main details of a technology demonstrator:
Length 1.25 m (max.)
Height 1.25 m (max.)
Width 0.30 m (max.) to 0.24 m (min.)
Number of external covering membranes 1
Number of water reception balls 42
Number of water storage balls 42
Number of colour indicator balls 40
Number of TB spiral springs 60
Number of hygrobicomposite spiral springs 20
Number of pairs of hairs 21
Number of transpirator rings 42

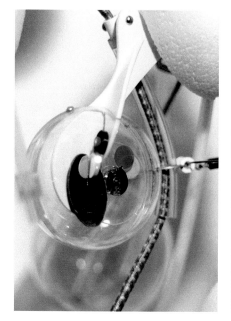
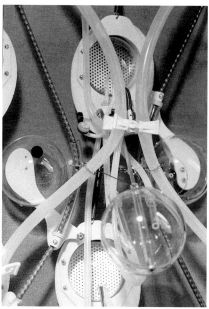

Polyreactive mechanomembrane: colour indicator ball on support arm |
Module tied in by two elastic bands | Overall view, rear side.

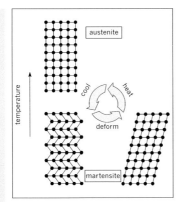

Phase change between high temperature phase (austenite) and low temperature phase (martensite). Deformation is reversed through warming.

shape memory alloys (SMA) › materials

Shape memory alloys (SMA), also called shape memory metals or memory metals, consist of at least two different metallic elements and have the property, after a thermomechanical treatment, to take up, reversibly and temperature-dependent, a shape they were given earlier. This effect relies on a repeatable phase change between two crystal structures. Above a critical temperature the metals have a hard, high-strength, austenitic crystal lattice structure, below this temperature it changes to a soft, easily deformable, martensitic crystal lattice structure. The crystal structures were named after the materials scientist Sir William Chandler Roberts-Austen (1843 to 1902) and the metallurgist Adolf Martens (1850 to 1914) respectively.

There are three different memory effects:

THERMAL MEMORY EFFECT (ONE-OFF EFFECT, ONE-WAY EFFECT):
If a shape memory alloy component is permanently mechanically deformed in the low temperature phase (martensite) and then heated above the transformation temperature, the crystal structure changes to form austenite, and the component takes up its original shape and retains that original shape even after subsequent cooling.

THERMAL MEMORY EFFECT (REPEATABLE EFFECT, TWO-WAY EFFECT):
In contrast to the one-time effect, here the component returns to the original shape on subsequent cooling. If the return to the original shape on cooling is caused by the action of an outside force, for example a spring or a weight, this is called an external (extrinsic) two-way effect; if it is caused by thermomechanical treatment of the component, it is called an intrinsic two-way effect.

MECHANICAL MEMORY EFFECT (SUPERELASTICITY, PSEUDOELASTICITY):
Some shape memory alloys are about 20 times more elastic at constant temperature than conventional metals. This is due to the mechanical change of the crystal structure.

The phenomenon of the shape memory effect was discovered in a gold cadmium alloy at the beginning of the 1930s by Swedish researcher Arne Ölander. The same effect was noticed in a copper-zinc alloy in 1956. In 1961 the strongest shape memory effect up to this day was discovered by the American Naval Ordnance Laboratory in a nickel-titanium alloy, which was given the commercial name of Nitinol to reflect the names of its constituent elements and its place of discovery.

Materials and components in use include:

BASIC ALLOYS
Nickel-titanium (NiTi, e.g. Nitinol), copper-zinc-aluminium (CuZnAl), iron-platinum (FePt), gold-cadmium (AuCd)
Alloying with other elements like copper or iron allows various properties to be influenced, such as the transformation temperature, the hysteresis range, the strength of the effect, long-term stability and mechanical properties of the alloy. If for example gold, hafnium or zircon is added to nickel-titanium alloys, then this produces alloys with higher transformation temperatures, such as are necessary for example to meet the safety requirements of the automobile industry. (after [5])

The following alloys are among those of interest in architecture:

NICKEL-TITANIUM (NiTi, E.G. NITINOL)
+ Market presence, can be made in large quantities, many years of practical use, wide range of applications, strong shape memory effect, better tensile strength and elongation at break compared with other SMAs, specific properties can be achieved by additional alloy elements, can also be supplied in small quantities.
− Relatively expensive compared with TB alloys.

COPPER-ZINC-ALUMINIUM (CuZnAl)
+ Relatively easy to machine compared with nickel-titanium alloys. Otherwise with the limitations as above.
− Weaker shape memory effect, poorer tensile strength and elongation at break compared with nickel-titanium alloys. Otherwise as above.

shape memory alloys (sma) › products

Shape memory alloys (SMA) have lost none of their fascination since their discovery. In conjunction with the increased interest in smart materials, the possibilities presented by shape memory effects are bringing out ideas from a wide range of professions on how SMAs could be used in everyday products.

Among the first users of SMAs was NASA, who developed a satellite dish that folded out under the influence of solar radiation. Today SMAs are used in air and space travel as decoupling mechanisms and tube connectors, e.g. for fuel pipes in satellites. Other fields of application include medicine, where stents are used to widen blood vessels, microsystem technology, measurement and control technology, electrical and automobile engineering. They have also found their first uses in the consumer goods sector and in functional textiles (see p. 16). In household electronic appliances these alloys are already replacing some TB components.

Plastics have also been developed that display similar behaviour when stimulated by light or temperature changes. Future research is likely to involve light-stimulated shape memory plastics (memory polymers), in particular in medical devices.

No market-ready products with SMAs have been developed for use in architecture yet, although the number of designs involving smart materials produced by universities has been on the increase for years. The following is an overview of the currently available semifinished products.

Raw or end products made from SMAs currently available include:

Wires and rods made from SMAs

SMA springs with superelasticity and corrosion-resistant chromium coating. | SMA springs with two-way effect.

FULL-SECTION SMA WIRES AND RODS
Nickel-titanium alloy wire is available in diameters of approx. 0.018 mm to 5 mm from stock, copper-zinc-aluminium alloy wire in diameters of approx. 1 mm upwards. They can be clamped at one or both ends, installed as endless, and weaved manually or mechanically, depending on the diameter and mesh size.
+ Depending on the shape memory effect they can be used as actuating and positioning drives to provide continuous, almost linear or discontinuous, sudden movements, can be used as active components in drives to create rotational movements and in textiles, as elastic elements/components and as structural components, relatively long actuator paths compared with piezoelectrically operated actuating and positioning drives; may have bending-, tension-, compression-, torsion- and shape-changing properties, silent. Otherwise as for alloys above.
− Relatively sluggish reaction times compared with e.g. piezoelectrically operated actuating and positioning drives. Otherwise as for alloys above.

SMA HOLLOW WIRES AND RODS (TUBES)

Nickel-titanium alloy tubes are available in diameters of approx. 0.200 mm to 4.520 mm from stock.

+ Quicker reaction times than full-section wires and rods, suitable for carrying liquids, which can provide additional or all of the heat stimulus. Otherwise as above.

– As above.

SMA SPRINGS

Are available as compression or tension springs in the dimensions listed above for wires and rods, can be clamped at one or both ends, guided through their centres or enclosed in a sleeve.

+ As above.

– As above.

SMA bands and sheets:

SMA BANDS AND STRIPS

Nickel-titanium alloy bands are available in thicknesses of approx. 0.013 mm to 0.410 mm from stock, can be clamped at one or both ends, used individually or in layers for multiplication of the effect, guided through their centres or enclosed in a sleeve.

+ As above.

– As above.

SMA SHEETS

Nickel-titanium alloys are available in thicknesses of approx. 0.200 mm to 1.000 mm and sizes of up to < 95.000 mm x 400.000 mm from stock, can be clamped at one or both ends or can be installed as circumferentially restrained.

+ Can be used as active components in self-healing and self-shaping surface-forming components, for example cladding. Otherwise with the limitations as above.

– Shape recovery performance is limited by geometry, only available in relatively small diameters. Otherwise with the limitations as above.

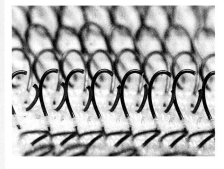

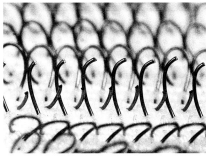

Technology by EADS: hook and loop fastener with nickel-titanium alloy hooks; normal state closed, open after the effect of heat.

Special shapes in SMAs:

SMA CLAMPS AND STENTS
Clamps and stents can be designed and manufactured to suit specific requirements. They can be installed and clamped in various ways depending on geometry and use; they can also be manufactured using laser cutting machines.
+ Complex two- and three-dimensional geometries can be created. Otherwise as above.
– Relatively expensive compared with standard shapes. Otherwise as above.

Currently available or developed SMA intermediate and end products include:

SMA variable connection devices:

HOOK AND LOOP FASTENERS
A technology demonstrator for a hook and loop fastener with nickel-titanium alloy hooks was designed and manufactured by the Corporate Research Centre (CRC) of EADS in Ottobrunn, Germany. It can be attached as strips or patches on stiff components and textiles, either mechanically, e.g. by sewing, or by adhesive.
+ Can be used to create reversible, complex, multi-dimensional connections, connections can be separated perpendicularly with no force and reformed again, can be used on various substrates in a number of ways. Otherwise as for nickel-titanium alloys above.
– Relatively expensive compared with conventional hook and loop fasteners, for as yet only at the technology demonstrator stage. Otherwise as for nickel-titanium alloys above.

The alloys perform differently depending on their composition, for example with respect to the number of possible change cycles and their corrosion resistance. Nickel-titanium alloys have somewhat better long-term stability than for example copper-zinc-aluminium alloys. All products should not be loaded up to their limits. Several components can be fitted in parallel and/or series to increase their performance especially when used as actuating or positioning drives.

Products currently in use in architecture and likely to become more relevant in future include:

RAW OR END PRODUCTS:

SMA WIRES, RODS, TUBES

SMA BANDS and SHEETS

SPECIAL SHAPES in SMAs

SMA ASSEMBLIES

INTERMEDIATE OR END PRODUCTS:

TUBE CONNECTION ELEMENTS MADE from SMA with one-way effect

ACTUATING and POSITIONING DRIVES made from or incorporating SMAs

CONTROL and REGULATING ELEMENTS made from or incorporating SMAs

SPRING ELEMENTS with variable spring force made from or incorporating SMAs

HOOK and LOOP FASTENERS made from SMAs

TEXTILES with SMA threads

Construction membranes with a tensegrity structure of SMA wires

PASSIVE STRUTS made from SMAs with pseudoelastic behaviour in bridges

shape memory alloys (sma) › projects

There are various possible uses of shape memory alloy (SMA) products in architecture. The type of shape memory effect determines their particular suitability. Already established in the automobile industry, tube connection elements made from SMAs with one-way effect could be used in the future in the construction of skeletal building elements such as lattice beams. On the grounds of cost they will be limited initially to relatively light constructions with small diameter members.

It would be feasible to install the previously described hook and loop fasteners as temperature-sensitive, variable connection elements in conjunction with changeable roofs, or changeable textiles for interiors, in order to allow them to have different light transmission properties at the contact points, e.g. transparent, opaque etc.

In Italy, a bridge has been built with passive struts made from SMAs with pseudoelastic properties. The SMA members are intended to attenuate any seismically induced forces in the structure.

In 1995 Anja-Natalie Richter, then a student at the Bartlett School, London, developed a smart membrane which integrated SMA wires into a tensegrity structure to create a room-forming, geometrically changing assembly. 2003 saw the first functioning technology demonstrators of textiles with interwoven SMA wires that were specifically designed for use as room dividers or curtains.

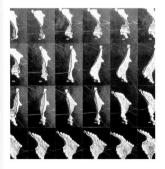

Construction membranes with a tensegrity structure of SMA wires (Nitinol): *smart membrane*, Anja-Natalie Richter.

shape memory interior textiles

Monosmart material | Monosmart application
Thermostrictive smart materials:
TEXTILES WITH SMA
Temperature-dependent kinetic structures

Yvonne Chan Vili, Great Britain
Textiles with SMA for use in rooms | Great Britain (2003)

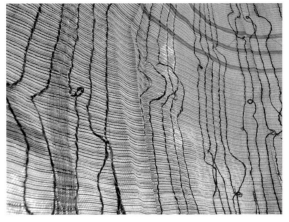

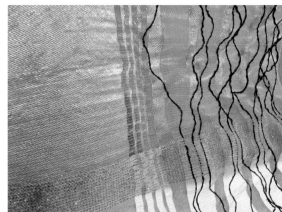

These structures are intended to be functional and have high aesthetic appeal: textiles with SMA threads for use in building interiors.

Yvonne Chan Vili has designed and manufactured several technology demonstrators in various patterns and colours. The professor at the School of Design at the University of Leeds used textiles woven from conventional threads and incorporated parallel strands of SMA wires at a few places in the surface for her *Shape Memory Interior Textiles*. This type of arrangement gives the temperature-sensitive wires adequate space for contraction while creating more or less pronounced linear or irregular structures, depending on the temperature.

This produces functional textiles suitable for black-out or privacy coverings for vertical, inclined or horizontal window and door openings, or as components of room divider and wall cladding systems.

Earlier forms included among others a curtain that could be installed inside a building in front of a roof window. For this curtain, a textile to allow temperature-dependent control of the amount of admitted light was produced with SMA wires and several horizontally running elongated openings. The openings would change their effective width throughout the day in response to room temperature and degree of folding.

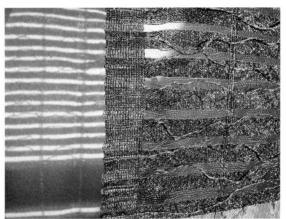

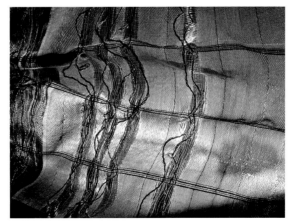

Shape Memory Interior Textiles: various designs of textiles incorporating SMA threads. | Actual application as a curtain. | Possible use as room divider.

ELECTROACTIVE SMART MATERIALS >
MATERIALS, PRODUCTS, PROJECTS

The inherent properties of electroactive smart materials allow them to reversibly change their shape in response to neighbouring electrical fields.

The following electroactive smart materials are currently of interest to architects:

ELECTROACTIVE POLYMERS (EAP)

Other electroactive smart materials not discussed in detail here include:

ELECTROSTRICTIVE PAPERS

ELECTROSTRICTIVE CERAMICS

ELECTROSTRICTIVE GRAFT ELASTOMERS

Electrostrictive ceramics include unpolarised lead-magnesium-niobate (PMN), which is also used in components in piezoelectric ceramics (PEC) (see piezoelectric ceramics/polymers (PEC, PEP), pp. 154 ff.)

electroactive polymers (EAP) › materials

Electroactive polymers (EAP) are polymers that are able to change their shape under electric stimulation. If the shape change is caused by electrostatic forces produced by electrical charges, the materials are called electronic EAPs, and if due to diffused ions, ionic EAPs. Electronic EAPs include dielectric EAPs; ionic EAPs include conductive polymers (CP).

Among the dielectric EAPs developed in recent years are conventional polymer films (acryl-based), which are designed to be stimulated by an electrical field like a flexible capacitor and therefore are coated on both sides with an elastical, electrically conductive layer of, for example, graphite powder. "After the application of an electrical voltage, the capacitor becomes electrically charged and the electrostatic attraction forces of the electrodes press the elastic polymer film together in the through-thickness direction, which causes it to expand laterally together with the coating. As soon as the capacitors are short-circuited, the electrostatic forces of the electrodes disappear and the elastic film contracts back to its original shape." [6]

EAP-based actuators that curve, expand or contract can be created through the appropriate choice of geometry, form of restraint and construction.

By the use of repeated layering in their construction, through the principle of winding and by combination, a wide variety of active, adaptive structures, including bender actuators, can be produced (see piezoelectric ceramics/polymers (PEC, PEP), pp. 154 ff.).

The development of EAPs goes back to 1880 and Röntgen's experiments with an elastic band. The band, which was fixed at one end and attached to a weight at the other, shortened when an electric charge was applied by an electrical field. In 1925 followed the development of electret, a piezoelectric polymer which reacts to a direct current electrical field (see piezoelectric ceramics/polymers (PEC, PEP), pp. 154 ff.). Later followed the development of polymers that could react to chemical, thermal, pneumatic, optical or magnetic influences. As early as 1949 the first polymers were stimulated by contact with acidic and alkaline solutions to contract and expand; they were based on Katchalsky's research into collagen filaments. EAPs were first considered insignificant because of their low output, and it was only in the last 15 years with the use of new materials and increasing success that they became of interest as smart materials.

Materials and components generally used include among others:

Schematic representation of the construction and functioning of an actuator made from dielectric elastomer film with electrodes applied to both sides (electronic EAP).

Electronic EAP components:

DIELECTRIC EAP
Organic dielectric elastomer film: e.g. acryl-based or silicon-based.
Inorganic electrodes made from electrically conductive particles: e.g. graphite, carbon black.

Ionic EAP components:

ELECTRICALLY CONDUCTIVE POLYMERS (CONDUCTIVE POLYMERS, CPS)
Organic conductors: e.g. polypyrrol-based (e.g. PPy-CF_3SO_3, PPy-TFSI).

Other electronic EAPs include:

FERROELECTRIC POLYMERS
Electrostrictive graft elastomers

Other ionic EAPs include:

IONIC POLYMER GELS (IPG)
Electrorheological fluids (ERF) (see p. 38)

The following component combinations are among those of interest in architecture:

ACRYL-BASED COMPONENTS WITH GRAPHITE
Commercially available, acryl-based transparent films coated on both sides with graphite as electrodes.
✚ Relatively simple to produce through the use of commercially available components, performance can be multiplied by multi-layering and winding (increased activation forces), relatively large changes of shape possible (expansions of up to 380%), wide range of uses.
▬ Not available in large quantities, relatively high activation voltage (kV) required, film is hygroscopic.

PPy-CF_3SO_3
Polypyrrol-based conductive composite polymer.
✚ Larger movement capacity than with TFSI as component, performance can be multiplied by layering or winding, wide range of uses.
▬ Not available in large quantities.

Acryl-based dielectric film.

PPy-TFSI	
Polypyrrol-based conductive composite polymer.	
+	Greater flexibility than can be achieved with CF_3SO_3 as component, performance can be multiplied by layering or winding, wide range of uses.
−	Not available in large quantities.

electroactive polymers (EAP) › products

Products incorporating electroactive polymers (EAP) are being developed all over the world. At the moment, dielectric EAPs require a very high voltage for activation (kV). One possible solution to this could be a future reduction in film thickness.

In the past, EAPs were mainly developed for trials and demonstrations because of their relatively large deformations and small actuation forces. Among these were trials in which bender actuators clamped on one side and incorporating EAPs were used as windscreen wiper blades. By combining several bender actuators it was furthermore possible to make gripping actuators. In recent years they have also been used in trials of artificial muscles. Future applications of EAPs are likely to include adaptive wing sections and elastic tubes that are able to change their local diameters.

In order to use EAPs as actuating and positioning drives (linear actuators, bender actuators) or as components of assemblies, existing products will have to be suitably adapted and will therefore have completely new properties. Actuating and positioning drives based on fibres, films, coils and composites are among the earlier types of devices that can be deformed along their longitudinal axes by electrical stimulation. If the selected EAP itself does not have a shape restoration effect, it can be provided by the addition of one or more components with this effect. Several of these basic components can be arranged in parallel or series to multiply their performance. The glued or mechanical bond between the components transmits forces and is permanent.

EAPs may be produced as raw, intermediate and end products, depending on the number of process steps and the intended purpose.

Technology by EMPA: Technology demonstrator of inflated dielectric elastomer film with electrodes attached on both sides (balloon actuator, electronic EAPs), not activated and activated. | *opposite:* Technology by EMPA: Technology demonstrator of a rocker driven by two EAP muscle pairs and able to perform mechanical work by alternately lifting two metal balls. | Robot with several linear actuators incorporating dielectric EAPs arranged in parallel, participating in an arm-wrestling competition at the SPIE Symposium (EAPAD) 2005 in San Diego. | Wound linear actuator ("artificial muscle") with dielectric EAPs.

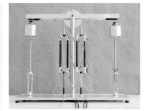

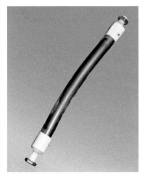

Products currently in use in architecture and likely to become more relevant in future include:

RAW OR END PRODUCTS:

EAP fibres

EAP strips and films

EAP coils

INTERMEDIATE OR END PRODUCTS:

ACTUATING and POSITIONING DRIVES made from or incorporating EAPs

SPRING ELEMENTS with variable/varying spring force made from or incorporating EAPs

ROBOTS with actuating and positioning drives incorporating EAPs

NEOPRENE MEMBRANE with EAP

Raw material or end products made from EAPs which have been developed and are available to some extent include:

FIBRES, YARNS (E.G. SANTA FE SCIENCE AND TECHNOLOGY)
They can be made from conductive polymers (CP), handled and processed with limitations similar to those of conventional yarns and textile fibres. Depending on the intended application they can also be given additional protective coatings and/or claddings.
+ Can be used to create linear movements by grouping actuating and positioning drives, various uses as fabrics. Otherwise as for PPy-CF$_3$SO$_3$ and PPy-TFSI above.
− Not universally available, relatively low movement capacity, low mechanical strength of individual yarns. Otherwise as for PPy-CF$_3$SO$_3$ and PPy-TFSI above.

STRIPS, FILMS (E.G. TECHNOLOGY BY EMPA)
They can be made from dielectric EAPs, installed as clamped at one or both ends, can be used to form casing components for example.
+ Can be used in medium temperatures ranges (< −20°C to > +50°C), can be grouped as actuating or positioning drives to produce linear movements, can be cut to size. Otherwise as for acryl-based components with graphite.
− No very small bevels or folds can be made. Otherwise as for acryl-based components with graphite.

COILS (E.G. TECHNOLOGY BY EAMEX)
They can be made out of conductive polymers (CPs) and can be installed as clamped at one end.
+ Can be used to create continuous linear movements by grouping actuating and positioning drives, and as spring elements. Otherwise as for PPy-CF$_3$SO$_3$ and PPy-TFSI above.
− Relatively low movement or spring capacity, low mechanical load capacity. Otherwise as for PPy-CF$_3$SO$_3$ and PPy-TFSI above.

These products should also not be loaded up to their limits. Depending on the product and design principle, it should be ensured that where layers of dielectric and electrically conductive materials are placed upon one another, they do not become separated by moisture entry. No water should be allowed to enter EAP actuators, as this could seriously reduce the dielectric strength of the hygroscopic films.

electroactive polymers (EAP) › projects

As it is only in recent years that products with adequate reversible and reproducible shape-changing properties have been developed and given that they are still mainly implemented as technology demonstrators, there are likely to be no products available for widespread use in the field of architecture in the foreseeable future, in particular as actuating or positioning drives. These drives are most likely to appear first as trials because new construction products require official approval, and this is normally a lengthy process. For the time being the existing available drives will continue to be used but perhaps with modifications or suitable connections, depending on future uses.

In the short term, electrically deformable, large surface-forming components could be made from EAP films to produce various textures in wall coverings or wallpaper.

BalnaeNY

Monosmart material | Monosmart application
Electroactive smart material:
NEOPRENE MEMBRANE WITH EAP
Kinetic structures responding to electromagnetic radiation

Bryan Boyer, USA
Electromagnetically sensitive thermal baths with kinetic surface-forming components | New York, USA (2003)

With his 2003 design, *BalnaeNY*, the American designer Bryan Boyer showed how the activities that arise in a certain built area can be used to enrich the experience for those who visit it through deformable walls and floors. In this particular case, Boyer applied his design to a fun bath in New York's busy SOHO district.

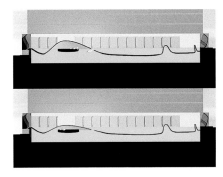

Boyer, then a student at Future Studio, a special department at the Rhode Island School of Design, proposed a system of sensors and actuators that would react dynamically to the various activities taking place in the course of a day. The electromagnetic radiation generated by people and their mobile phones, motor vehicles etc. is picked up and converted into kinetic spatial changes by an EAP. The material is integrated into an additional intermediate neoprene floor close to the water surface of the pool, into the walls of the shower enclosures and into the facade. For example, depending on the time of day, part of the intermediate floor containing a grid of EAP strips will take up a wave profile and emerge to a greater or lesser extent above the water's surface, thus forming a walk-in cave. The shower walls can adopt a spiral shape in plan when they function as a shower enclosure and offer privacy, or they can take up another shape to function as a splash guard.

The walls forming the narrow sides of the pool also consist of EAPs and shape themselves, depending on the activities taking place, into variously sized niches that can be used as individual sauna areas. The niches may project into the street space to various extents so that the activity is also visible from outside the building.

BalnaeNY: perspective view from above of the swimming pool with the emerging and submerging wave profile of the neoprene membrane. | Scenario of deforming sauna walls projecting into street space | Section through swimming pool with neoprene membrane | View into interior of cave. | Individual sauna areas. | Unwinding shower enclosures.

colour- and optically changing smart materials

Colour- and optically changing smart materials include materials and products that are able to reversibly change their colour and/or optical properties in response to one or more stimuli through the external influence of light, temperature, compression, an electrical or magnetic field and/or a chemical stimulus.

The currently available colour- and optically changing smart materials can be differentiated according to their triggering stimuli as follows:

PHOTOCHROMIC SMART MATERIALS
These materials change their colour when excited by the effect of light (electromagnetic energy).
THERMOCHROMIC, THERMOTROPIC SMART MATERIALS
These materials change their colour and/or optical properties when excited by the effect of temperature (thermal energy).
MECHANOCHROMIC (E.G. PIEZOCHROMIC, TRIBOCHROMIC) SMART MATERIALS
These materials change their colour when excited by the effect of compression, tension or friction (mechanical energy).
ELECTROCHROMIC, ELECTROOPTIC (E.G. IONOCHROMIC) SMART MATERIALS
These materials change their colour and/or optical properties when excited by the effect of electrical fields, electrons or ions (electrical energy).
CHEMOCHROMIC (E.G. GASCHROMIC, HALOCHROMIC, SOLVATOCHROMIC, HYGRO-/ HYDROCHROMIC) SMART MATERIALS
These materials change their colour and/or optical properties when excited by the effect of a chemical environment (chemical energy), e.g. hydrogen, oxygen, salt content (pH value), a solution or water.

The general term, chromogenic smart materials, is also used.

Of the above smart materials, due to their availability and other factors, such as the anticipated long-term stability, the following are of interest for architectural applications and will be dealt with in more detail below: photochromic, thermochromic, thermotropic, electrochromic and electrooptic smart materials. An application of hygro-/hydrochromic smart materials can be found elsewhere (see p. 24).

Assuming further development and market placement, piezochromic, gaschromic and halochromic smart materials could gain in importance in the near future.

housewarming III: room installation with thermochromic wall and seat surfaces.

**PHOTOCHROMIC SMART MATERIALS >
MATERIALS, PRODUCTS, PROJECTS**

Their inherent properties enable them to react to light (visible light, UV light, IR light; electromagnetic radiation) by changing their colour.

The following photochromic smart materials are currently of interest to architects:

PHOTOCHROMIC MATERIALS (PC)

These materials and products include:

PHOTOCHROMIC PIGMENTS

PHOTOCHROMIC GLASS

PHOTOCHROMIC PLASTICS

Photochromic plastics are also known as photochromic polymers (PCP)

photochromic materials (PC) › materials

Photochromic materials (PC), photochromics and UV-sensitive materials are materials or components that are able to reversibly change their colour in response to light.

Photochromism describes the reversible conversion of materials or components between two forms A and B, each with different absorption spectra. The conversion is triggered, in one or both directions, by the absorption of electromagnetic radiation. The thermodynamically more stable form A is transformed by irradiation into form B. The reverse reaction may be thermal (T-type photochromism) or photochemical (P-type photochromism) (according to: [7]).

The following applies to certain organic PCs: if form A is colourless or slightly yellow and form B is coloured then this is called positive photochromism, which is the most common case. In less frequent cases if form A is coloured and form B is colourless, then the colour is bleached by light and this is called negative photochromism.

Two mechanisms may be involved in the process: with the one-photon mechanism, B is formed from the initial singlet or the triplet excited state or both, whilst with the two-photon mechanism, B is formed by the absorption of two photons, which can be simultaneous or step-wise (sequential), and the resulting upper excited state. Accordingly, the phenomenon is referred to as one-photon or two-photon photochromism.

In 1899 a photochromic effect was discovered by Markwald in tetrachloronaphthaline in the solid state, which established the term phototropy for what he saw as a merely physical phenomenon. In Israel in 1950, Hirshberg suggested the term in use today, photochromism, which is derived from Greek. Fatigue-proof derivates of spirooxazines and chromenes were developed in the 1980s. In 2001 Japanese scientists at the National Institute of Advanced Industrial Science and Technology developed a new photochromic glass based on silver ions and nitrate without the use of environment- and health-damaging halogens. In 2004 a photo-electrochromic system consisting of a dye solar cell with an electrochromic component was developed in Germany at the Fraunhofer Institute for Solar Energy Systems, Freiburg.

Materials and components generally used include among others:

ORGANIC COMPOUNDS
Naphthopyranes, spiropyranes, spirooxazines (e.g. spironaphthoxazines), spirodihydroindolizines, chromenes, diarylethenes, fulgides, azo compounds, bakteriorhodopsin (BR)

INORGANIC COMPOUNDS
Silver halides (e.g. silver bromide (AgBr), silver chloride (AgCl), silver iodide (AgI))

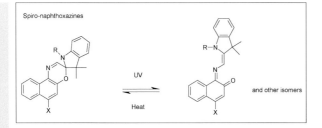

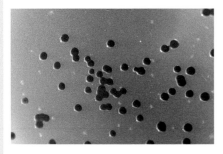

Diagram of the chemical structure of naphthopyrane and spironaphthoxazines before and after the exposure to UV light. | Clones of halobacterium salinarum on an agar plate. This contains the information for the production of the modified BR. | Different colours of BR pigments.

The following PCs are among those of interest in architecture:

SPIROPYRANES, SPIRODIHYDROINDOLIZINES

Organic chemical compounds, solid at +20°C. They react to the influence of visible and UV light by undergoing a reversible colour change from colourless or slightly yellow (form A) to coloured, e.g. blue or red (form B). Some spiropyranes show the opposite behaviour (negative photochromism) and are thermochromic (see thermochromic smart materials, pp. 80 ff.). Available as powders.

+ Market presence, can be made in large quantities, can be used in low to medium temperatures (−40°C to +150°C), relatively wide absorption spectrum (form A: approx. 350 nm to 450 nm, form B: approx. 500 nm to 100 nm wavelength), relatively large number of possible cycles of colour change (> 105), form B available in all spectral colours, soluble in ethanol, toluene, ether, ketones and esters among other liquids, also soluble in water by substitution (e.g. for the manufacture of dyes), non-toxic, biologically degradable, relatively inexpensive compared with BR.

− None known.

NAPHTHOPYRANES, SPIROOXAZINES (E.G. SPIRONAPHTHOXAZINES), DIARYLETHENES

As above.

+ Can be used in low to high temperatures (−40°C to +250°C), relatively wide absorption spectrum (form A: approx. 380 nm to 780 nm, form B: approx. 380 nm to 295 nm wavelength), relatively large number of possible cycles of colour change (> 106), relatively good lightfastness compared with spiropyranes. Otherwise as above.

− Not soluble in water.

BACTERIORHODOPSIN (BR)

A protein isolated from the cell membrane, the so-called purple membrane, of the salt-loving archaebacteria of the species halobacterium salinarum. Solid at +20°C. Uses include the display, storage and processing of optical information. Currently, optical films are among the products manufactured from Bacteriorhodopsin (BR). It reacts to the influence of light by undergoing a reversible colour change from violet to yellow. The time over which this takes place can be controlled and influenced by the genetic modification of the protein. Available as powders and aqueous solutions (suspensions). Currently at the market introduction phase.

+ Can be made in large quantities, can be used in low to medium temperatures (−20°C to +80° or +120°C, in aqueous solution or in dry form respectively), relatively wide absorption spectrum (form A: 570 nm, form B: 410 nm wavelength), relatively large number of possible cycles of colour change (> 106), relatively good lightfastness compared with spiropyranes, water-soluble, non-toxic, biologically degradable.

− Little market presence, form A not transparent, available as a powder in one colour only, relatively expensive compared with spiropyranes or silver bromide.

Technology by James Robinson:
illustration of the positive
photochromic effect in sunglasses
with plastic lenses incorporating
organic PCs. | Sunglasses and six
plastic lenses incorporating
organic PCs (ophthalmic lenses)
before and after excitement with
light.

SILVER BROMIDE (AgBr)
Sometimes called bromic silver. An inorganic chemical compound formed as the greenish-yellow precipitate of the reaction between silver salts, usually silver nitrate, with an aqueous solution of a bromide salt, often calcium bromide. Solid at +20°C. The compound is used in photography as the light-sensitive component of emulsions on films and in other light-sensitive coatings, for example photochromic glass. Decomposes under the influence of high energy shortwave blue or violet light into black-coloured silver and bromine. Doping with sensitising dyes allows also lower energy light colours such as red light to be absorbed.
+ Market presence, can be made in large quantities, many years of practical use, can be used in low to high temperatures (< –20°C to > +250°C), relatively large number of possible cycles of colour change (> 105), relatively good lightfastness compared with organic PCs such as spiropyranes, relatively inexpensive compared with BR.
– Relatively narrow absorption spectrum, form B only available in one colour (various shades of grey), not resistant to rust and other corrosion products in contact with metals, toxic, problematic recyclability.

In addition to the above materials and components, the Fraunhofer Institute for Solar Energy Systems has developed a new photochromic system in which electrochromic tungsten oxide is used: this is described in the appropriate section (see electrochromic/-optic materials (EC, EO), pp. 89 ff.).

photochromic materials (PC) › products

One of the most widely known applications of photochromic materials (PC) are self-colouring sunglasses, which have been on the market for over 20 years. By means of applied or embedded inorganic silver halide crystals the lenses change to various shades of grey, or brown, by the addition of gold or palladium, depending on the intensity of light. Other colours, including red and blue, can be produced by the addition of organic PCs, such as spirodihydroindolizines.

A number of different chromogenic products for children, some of them photochromic, were brought on to the market at the beginning of the 1990s by Mattel, a large US-American toy manufacturer.

Apart from toys, PCs find use in other consumer goods as well; they can also be used in control technology. In the meantime, dental sealant materials (fissure sealants) based on spirodihydroindolizines have appeared on the market. They change colour from transparent to blue after a few seconds of exposure to a polymerisation lamp and provide quality control [8].

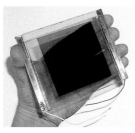

A promising application of BR could be in aqueous solutions or as dyes on, for example, films for the display, storage or processing of optical information.

The following products made from or incorporating PCs are among those of interest for architectural applications:

Dyes made from photochromic organic compounds:

DYES MADE FROM PC (REVERSACOL, TECHNOLOGY BY JAMES ROBINSON)
Photochromic powder made from naphthopyranes or spironaphthoxazines. They can be added to inks and paints as dopants or to various solvents such as ethanol and toluene. They can also be incorporated into plastics, for example thermoplastics such as PE, PP, PVC, EVA, PVB, PMMA, and duroplastics like PUR and be thermally treated for extrusion, casting or injection moulding into various forms.
+ Market presence, can be made in large quantities, can be used in low to high temperatures (–40°C to +250°C, depending on the matrix among other parameters), largely lightfast, good batchability, can be embedded in different plastics. Otherwise as for naphthopyranes, spirooxazines (e.g. spironaphthoxazines), diarylethenes.
− Relatively expensive. Otherwise as for naphthopyranes, spirooxazines (e.g. spironaphthoxazines), diarylethenes.

Paints incorporating photochromic organic compounds:

PAINTS INCORPORATING PC, DISPERSION-BASED (E.G. WITH REVERSACOL DYES, TECHNOLOGY BY JAMES ROBINSON)
They can be applied by brush, roller or spray to surfaces such as wood, plastic, textiles, paper, cardboard, concrete and masonry. Otherwise as above.
+ High flexibility, good adhesion. Otherwise as above.
− As above.

Other products incorporating photochromic organic compounds include:

GRANULATES INCORPORATING PCs
THREADS INCORPORATING PCs

Technology by Chromatic Technologies Inc.: photochromic paint (DynaColor, "Photochromic Wet Slurry") before and during excitement with light. | Photochromic BR-based paints produced by chemical derivatisation. | Photochromic BR-based film. Information can be written on it using a light pen. | Technology by Fraunhofer Institute for Solar Energy Systems: technology demonstrators of photochromic and photo-electrochromic glass systems before and after excitement with light. | *opposite:* Schematic representation of the construction of photochromic and photo-electrochromic glass systems.

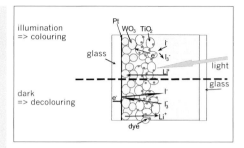

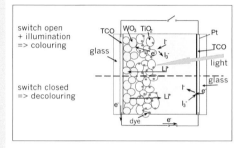

Products currently used in architecture include:

RAW OR END PRODUCTS:

DYES made from PCs (e.g. naphthopyranes, spironaphthoxazines) (e.g. Reversacol dyes, technology by James Robinson)

SUSPENSIONS incorporating PCs (e.g. BR)

DYES (e.g. inks, printing inks) incorporating PCs (e.g. naphthopyranes, spironaphthoxazines) (e.g. DynaColor, technology by Chromatic Technologies Inc.)

GRANULATES incorporating PCs (e.g. naphthopyranes, spironaphthoxazines)

THREADS incorporating PCs (e.g. naphthopyranes, spironaphthoxazines)

INTERMEDIATE OR END PRODUCTS:

PAPERS incorporating PCs, e.g. photochromic dyes

FILMS incorporating PCs, e.g. photochromic dyes

TEXTILES incorporating PCs, e.g. photochromic yarns

GLASS SYSTEMS incorporating PCs (e.g. silver halides)

Glass incorporating electrochromic inorganic compounds:

GLASS SYSTEMS INCORPORATING ELECTROCHROMIC MATERIALS (EC) (TECHNOLOGY BY FRAUNHOFER INSTITUTE OF SOLAR ENERGY SYSTEMS)
Photochromic system consisting of electrochromic tungsten oxide and a dye solar cell. Under the influence of light, electrons in the solar cell layer become excited and are injected into the tungsten oxide. At the same time cations from the electrolyte are taken into the layer and the tungsten oxide turns blue. During darkness decolouring takes place by recombination reactions. The photo-electrochromic version can be controlled by the user by means of a switch.
+ Suitable for darkening rooms, largely lightfast, can be installed in conjunction with adjacent conventional glazing, thus allowing clean details, relatively easy to use, no external electricity supply required. Otherwise with the limits mentioned above for tungsten oxide and dye solar cells.
– Lack of market presence, can be made in small quantities only, higher costs of replacement of damaged panes, relatively heavy, with resulting higher installation costs, no electrochromic or dye coatings can be applied to the edge of cells, hence edge covering is necessary. Otherwise with the limits mentioned above for tungsten oxide and dye solar cells.

Other products incorporating photochromic organic compounds include:

GLASS SYSTEMS INCORPORATING PCS (E.G. SILVER HALIDES)

The use of organic compounds such as naphthopyranes, spirooxazines (e.g. spironaphthoxazines) and diarylethenes allows products to be made that have relatively good long-term light stability, in terms of their colourfastness, for example. This can be increased by further additives, including UV absorbers, antioxidants, HALS (hindered amine light stabilisers). At the moment in this context, work is on-going with encapsulated dyes, which will probably respond less spontaneously. Toxic products such as those with layers of silver halides should be used as little as possible.

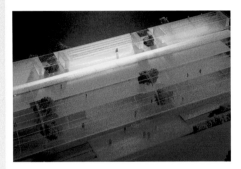

photochromic materials (PC) › projects

Until recent years there had been very few realised applications of photochromic materials (PC) in the fields of art (see p. 24) or architecture. Although the use of self-colouring glass in windows or facades is an obvious application, it has not been successful so far because of its inadequate long-term behaviour, sensitivity to heat and relatively high manufacturing costs. Accordingly, there are currently no known large-scale uses of these systems. Among the first projects involving PCs in a building envelope was the entry from Becker Gewers Kühn & Kühn Architects for the 1992 design competition for the *Museum of Modern Art* in Munich.

Since that time a number of other applications incorporating PCs have been proposed, particularly in the universities. They range from UV-sensitive wallpapers to textiles that are further processed into clothing or room textiles. While in the beginning the emphasis was on the aesthetics of the colour change, researchers are currently seeking to let these products take on further functions, such as the indication of energy state or time, or of changes in surface temperatures.

Model of a photochromatic glazed building envelope: *Museum of Modern Art, Munich*, by Becker Gewers Kühn & Kühn Architects.

Appearing Pattern Wallpaper

> Monosmart material | Polysmart application
> Colour- and optically changing smart material:
> **PHOTOCHROMIC DYE (INK)**
> Indication of UV light and time through colour change

Interactive Institute: Power Studio, Sweden
Wallpaper | Sweden (2005)

The *Appearing Pattern Wallpaper* project by the Interactive Institute's Power Studio in Eskilstuna seeks to raise awareness of energy forms that show themselves in less obvious ways than, for example, electric current. The institute works with others, including designers and manufacturers, on energy-related project themes.

For their project STATIC! designers Sofia Lagerkvist, Charlotte von der Lancken, Anna Lindgren and Katja Sävström developed a wallpaper with UV-sensitive inks, which can reversibly change from a monochromic to a bichromic red under the influence of light.

Appearing Pattern Wallpaper is intended to demonstrate to the observer in a poetic way how everyday objects can change over time under the influence of only subliminally perceived forms of energy.

Appearing Pattern Wallpaper: patterns (shown here in three sequential photographs) gradually changing during the absorption of UV light, left monochromic, right bichromic with the fully developed pattern.

THERMOCHROMIC AND THERMOTROPIC SMART MATERIALS
MATERIALS, PRODUCTS, PROJECTS

Their inherent properties enable them to react to temperature (thermal energy) by reversibly changing their colour and/or their optical characteristics.

The following thermochromic and thermotropic smart materials are currently of interest to architects:

THERMOCHROMIC MATERIALS (TC)

THERMOTROPIC MATERIALS (TT)

These materials and products include among others:

THERMOCHROMIC PIGMENTS

THERMOCHROMIC GLASS

THERMOTROPIC GLASS

THERMOCHROMIC PLASTICS

Thermochromic plastics are also known as thermochromic polymers (TCP).

thermochromic/-tropic materials (TC, TT) › materials

Thermochromic materials (TC) and thermochromics are materials or components that are able to reversibly change their colour in response to light. In contrast, thermotropic materials (TT) and thermotropics are materials or components that are able to reversibly change their optical characteristics (e.g. transparency) in response to temperature.

Certain liquid crystals that do not change directly from the crystalline to the liquid state when heated but go through one or more intermediate phases are classed as thermochromic materials, among others. In these phases they have directionally dependent physical properties, such as those found in crystals, yet they move like liquids. These phases are also known as mesomorphs.

In 1909, Prague chemist Hans Meyer observed thermochromic behaviour in certain organic compounds. An explanation for this phenomenon was not found until E. Harnik and G.M.J. Schmidt, and J.F.D. Mills and S.C. Nyburg published several articles about thermochromism in 1954 and 1963 respectively in the *Journal of the Chemical Society*, London. In 2003 in Germany, the Fraunhofer Institute for Applied Polymer Research in Golm near Berlin succeeded in developing microencapsulated thermochromic composites incorporated in various plastics, and a form of thermotropic solar protection.

Thermochromic materials and components generally used include among others:

ORGANIC COMPOUNDS
Cholesteric liquid crystals (e.g. cholesterylesters), leuco dyes (e.g. spiropyranes, fulgides).

INORGANIC COMPOUNDS
Metal oxides (e.g. vanadium oxide (VaO), vanadium tungsten oxide (VaWO), zinc oxide (ZnO), bismuth oxide (BiO), copper oxide (CuO)).
Metal iodides (e.g. mercury(II)-iodide).

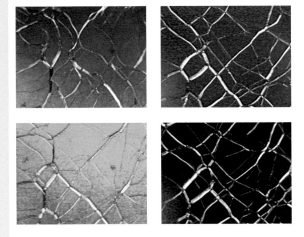

Choleristic compound cholesteryl-pelargonate at different temperatures (75° C, 76° C, 77° C, 79° C).

Thermochromic materials or components also include:

MINERALS
Rutil, thermochromic gemstones.

Thermotropic materials and components in use include among others:

ORGANIC COMPOUNDS
Polymer blends (e.g. polystyrene-co-HEMA/polypropylenoxide), lyotropic liquid crystals, resins, phase change materials (PCM) (e.g. paraffin).

HYBRID ORGANIC-INORGANIC COMPOUNDS
Hydrogels.

INORGANIC COMPOUNDS
Phase change materials (PCM) (e.g. salt hydrates).

The following TCs/TTs could be of interest in the field of architecture:

CHOLESTERIC LIQUID CRYSTALS (E.G. CHOLESTERYLESTERS)
Various organic compounds such as cholesterylesters. They react to a continuous temperature rise by changing colour from black through red, orange, yellow, green, blue to violet and back again to black.
Market presence, can be made in large quantities, can be used in low to medium temperatures (< –20°C to > +100°C), a reasonable number of cycles of possible changes of colour, suitable for precise applications, non-toxic.
Special manufacturing technology required, relatively low colour intensity, black background required to maximise the colour effect, relatively expensive.

LEUCO DYES (E.G. SPIROPYRANES, FULGIDES)
See products.

Technology by Chromatic Technologies Inc.: thermochromic paints (type DynaColor, switching at 31°C or at 45°C, "thermochromic UV screen").

LYOTROPIC LIQUID CRYSTALS
Various organic compounds. The mesophases can only be formed in mixtures. They react to a temperature rise by reversibly changing their optical characteristics from almost transparent to translucent (milky-white turbidity). They can be used in thermotropic layers, for example as solar protection.
+ Can be made in large quantities, can be used in low to high temperatures (< –30°C to > +120°C), relatively large number of possible cycles of changes between turbidity and clarity, relatively high transparency when switched off (approx. 90%), a relatively large proportion of NIR and IR radiation is reflected, non-toxic.
– Lack of market presence.

The use of phase change materials (PCM) in thermotropic layers in more complex systems is also interesting and is dealt with in more detail in the relevant chapter (see phase change materils (PCM) pp. 165 ff.), where a further thermotropic system is described.

thermochromic/-tropic materials (тc, тт) › products

Towards the end of the 1900s, a number of consumer products were enhanced with thermochromic characteristics and brought on to the market. The most well known include the mood rings from the 1970s, which can still be found on sale today. Also known in this context are toothbrushes made from coloured plastic that undergo a reversible colour change at the contact points where they have been held in the hand, or drinking vessels or straws that change colour when in contact with hot or cold drinks.

One of the first developments in the field of thermotropic products were switching hydrogels that are enclosed between glass substrates and have impressive optical characteristics. However, processing them under industrial conditions has proven too costly. A new use has been developed by the German Fraunhofer Institute for Applied Polymer Research in Golm near Berlin, in which solar protection based on phase change reversibly changes from almost transparent (90%) to translucent.

The following products made from or incorporating TCs and TTs are of interest for architectural applications:

Technology by Alsa Corporation: colour changes of a thermochromic paint (Xposures) on contact with water as the heat carrier. | Functioning of two thermochromic paints set to 31°C (Eclipse), each of which were mixed with one concentrate (candy red or candy yellow). As a result, e.g. on bodily contact, they change from black to red or from black to yellow respectively instead of from black to white.

Technology by Fraunhofer Institute for Applied Polymer Research: powdered microencapsulated TCs (composites), capable of being extruded and used as dopants in various plastics. | Thermoplastics: extruded thermochromic polymer film; highly transparent extruded thermochromic polymer film, switching temperature +72°C to +74°C. | Extruded thermochromic polymer strings. | Duroplastics: moulded thermochromic disc. | Thermochromic polymer material, showing different colours at different temperatures. | Hydrogels: thermochromic polymer gel. | Thermochromic polymer gel heated in a waterbath. Highly transparent in all phases.

Dyes made from thermochromic organic compounds:

LEUCO DYES INCORPORATING TC
Powdered microencapsulated thermochromic dyes made from, e.g. encapsulated spiro-pyranes or fulgides. They react to a temperature rise by reversibly changing colour from transparent to coloured, e.g. violet. The colour change takes place only when incorporated in a matrix, e.g. plastic.
+ Market presence, can be made in large quantities, can be used in low to medium temperatures (< –20°C to > +130°C), a reasonable number of cycles of possible changes of colour, non-toxic.
– Not particularly suitable for precise applications, relatively expensive.

Paints with thermochromic organic compounds:

PAINTS INCORPORATING TC AS PART OF A PAINT SYSTEM (ECLIPSE, TECHNOLOGY BY ALSA CORPORATION)
Monochromic colour changers, which consist of organic compounds dissolved in a liquid carrier; the organic compounds switch between black or blue to white and back again, depending on temperature. Can be applied by brush, roller or spray to surfaces such as metal, wood, glass, plastic, fabric and leather. Available as powder or paint.
+ Market presence, can be used in low to medium temperatures (< –20°C to > +80°C), relatively good mechanical load capacity compared with earlier products, good adhesion, good dirt resistance, simple to clean, resistance to wear with an additional protective lacquer, relatively good UV light resistance compared with earlier products, can be processed with other decorative paints and concentrates on the same basis, which enables other high temperature paints to be produced.
– Only available in two colours.

PAINTS INCORPORATING TC AS PART OF A PAINT SYSTEM (XPOSURES, TECHNOLOGY BY ALSA CORPORATION)
Polychrome colour changers that consist of liquid crystals dissolved in a liquid carrier; the liquid crystals change from an initial colour (e.g. blue) through a variety of other colours (brown, yellow, violet and green) and back again, depending on the temperature. Can be applied by brush, roller or spray to surfaces such as metal, wood, glass, plastic, fabric and leather. Available as paint only.
+ Eight different colours available, can be processed with other decorative paints and concentrates on the same basis. Otherwise as above and for liquid crystals.
– As for liquid crystals above.

Plastics incorporating thermochromic organic compounds:

MICROENCAPSULATED TC (COMPOSITES) (TECHNOLOGY BY FRAUNHOFER INSTITUTE FOR APPLIED POLYMER RESEARCH)
TCs that are microencapsulated, e.g. with transparent polymers; often powdered thermochromic composites. Can be incorporated as dopants into various plastics, e.g. in thermoplastics such as PE, PP, PVC, PES, ABS, PA, PC, PMMA, duroplastics such as PES, PUR and in paints, coatings and resins. Can be heat-treated for extrusion, casting or injection moulding into various shapes. They are currently in the development phase (technology demonstrators).
+ Can be made in large quantities, can be used in low to medium temperatures (−20°C to +100°C), largely lightfast, good batchability, can be embedded in various plastics, can be made into relatively large, uniformly coloured moulded parts and films, resistant to compression and temperature.
− Lack of market presence.

Products currently used in architecture include:

RAW OR END PRODUCTS:

LEUCO DYES incorporating TCs

PAINTS incorporating TCs as part of a paint system (Eclipse, technology by Alsa Corporation)

PAINTS incorporating TCs as part of a paint system (Xposures, technology by Alsa Corporation)

DYES (e.g. inks, printing inks) incorporating TCs (e.g. naphthopyranes, spironaphthoxazines) (e.g. DynaColor, technology by Chromatic Technologies Inc.)

MICROENCAPSULATED TCs (compounds) (technology by Fraunhofer Institute for Applied Polymer Research)

THREADS incorporating TCs (technology by Fraunhofer Institute for Applied Polymer Research)

Hydrogels incorporating TCs (technology by Fraunhofer Institute for Applied Polymer Research)

INTERMEDIATE OR END PRODUCTS:

PAPERS incorporating TCs, e.g. thermochromic dyes

FILMS incorporating TCs, e.g. thermochromic dyes

TEXTILES incorporating TCs, e.g. thermochromic yarns

GLASS SYSTEMS incorporating TTs (technology by Fraunhofer Institute for Applied Polymer Research)

thermochromic/-tropic materials (TC, TT) › projects

Applications involving thermochromic materials (TC) are more common than applications involving photochromic materials (PC). This applies as much to the fields of art and design as it does in architecture.

Among the first architectonic applications was a wall covered with a thermochromic paint in the Musée d'Art Moderne de la Ville de Paris by the German artist Sigmar Polke in 1988. Other artists and architects have since accepted the material and some of their works have included walls coated with thermochromic latex paints.

In addition, thermochromic components have been incorporated into a small number of furnishing items. In addition to new textiles that are used e.g. as table covers (see p. 22) and as wall coverings, room dividers or curtains, the first ceramic sanitary fittings such as wash basins and baths have been coated with appropriately sensitive dyes.

It is hoped in particular that thermotropic layers in e.g. glass systems will become an important tool for autonomously regulating the amount of light entering buildings. The use of TCs to indicate energy consumption also appears promising. The Power Studio of the Swedish Interactive Institute used TCs as part of its STATIC! project. In 2005, conventional ceramic wall tiles in a shower were given a floral decoration of multi-coloured thermochromic stickers. During each shower the dyes reacted, above a certain temperature, to the heat of the shower water by gradually decolouring and hence indicating the intensity of the shower, its duration and consumption of hot water.

Technology by Alsa Corporation: wash basin with thermochromic coating, initially black. | *opposite:* Technology by Fraunhofer Institute for Applied Polymer Research: behaviour of a thermotropic glass system as solar protection, based on reversible temperature-dependent phase transitions from transparent to translucent.

Thermowall

Monosmart material | Monosmart application
Colour- and optically changing smart material:
**THERMOCHROMIC PAINT (LIQUID CRYSTALS WITH A
SYNTHETIC BINDER)**
Indication of temperature differences (weather)
by colour change

Sigmar Polke, Germany
Wall installation | Musée d'Art Moderne de la Ville de
Paris, ARC, Paris, France (1988)

Two years after completing his *Hydrowand* for the German
pavilion at the XLII. Biennale in Venice the artist covered a
convex-curved wall with a large area of temperature-sensitive, colour-changing paint composed of liquid crystals and
a synthetic binder.

Through the use of three different types of liquid crystal that
changed colour over three different temperature ranges, the
Thermowand was meant to show the daily path of the sun by
reacting to the sunlight falling upon it.

The thermochromic dispersion paint used liquid crystal substances specifically selected to cover the temperature ranges
20°C to 22°C, 20°C to 25°C and 27°C to 33°C. The canvass
for his painting was a damp-proof aluminium membrane
glued to the wall. The paint contained toluene. It was therefore poisonous and had to be applied wearing a breathing
mask. The possible colour spectrum ranged from black
(cold, < 20°C) through violet-red, red, yellow, yellow-green
and green-blue to turquoise (warm, > 26°C).

The plan was that the roof construction would create a permanently changing "shadow drawing". As the sunlight did
not manage to reach the *Thermowand* as planned, an infra-
red lamp was installed to demonstrate how the wall
worked.

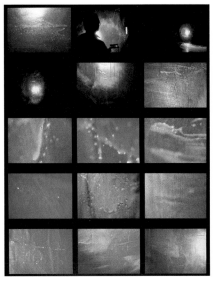

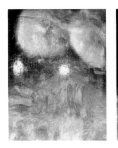

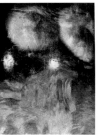

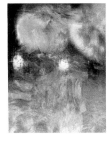

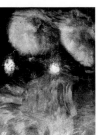

Thermowand: wall with the applied thermochromic paint in the
cold state (black). | Detailed photograph of paint coatings at
different temperatures.

housewarming III

Monosmart material | Monosmart application
Colour- and optically changing smart material:
LATEX PAINT WITH THERMOCHROMIC PIGMENTS
Indication of temperature differences by colour change

J. Mayer H., Germany
Room installation | Galerie magnusmüller, Berlin,
Germany (2005)

The Berlin architect and designer J. Mayer H. has exhibited
works incorporating thermochromic paints at several international exhibitions. A version of his installation IN HEAT,
which could be seen at Henry Urbach Architecture gallery,
New York, from April to May 2005, was created for the
Galerie magnusmüller to be on display from 17 September
to 10 November 2005.

housewarming III with its intensively pink-coloured, horizontally running, jagged bands and isolated thermosensitive,
brown polygons on the white walls of the gallery is reminiscent of the colour experiments seen at the end of the 1960s.
Unlike the rigorous interpretation of this concept in IN HEAT,
the ceilings and floors were left blank. Through the possibility of interaction with the room, J. Mayer H. develops further
Friedrich Kielser's idea of melding architecture and art with
the observers by having them become part of the exhibit.
Visitors can leave temporary images of their presence by
touching the thermosensitive areas.

The thermochromic paint pigment was set for the human
body temperature and decolours where touched. Originally
developed by NASA to signal overheating of mechanical
parts, the pigment was added to ordinary latex wall paint for
interior application. The idea of using a similar thermosensitive paint on exterior surfaces, for example as a self-darken-
ing exterior paint that would heat up in winter by absorbing
sunlight, was rejected due to high manufacturing costs and
inadequate UV resistance.

housewarming III: room installation.

chronos chromos concrete

Monosmart material | Monosmart application
Colour- and optically changing smart material:
CONCRETE WITH THERMOCHROMIC PIGMENTS
Displays of graphics and characters through temperature-dependent
colour changes triggered by electric current

Chris Glaister, Afshin Mehin, Tomas Rosen, Great Britain
Thermochromic concrete | Great Britain (2004)

Students at the Innovation Unit of the Royal College of Art (RCA) in London
developed a thermochromic concrete with which it was possible to use concrete as a display surface. Graphics and alphanumeric characters were created on the surface by means of electric currents. This was done by adding
thermochromic inks to the concrete and applying heat directly by current-
carrying nickel-chromium wires. Local colour changes are produced on the
surface, which may appear in the shape of dots, lines or patches depending
on the spacing of the wires.

As an alternative to direct heating, the colour changes can also be produced
by indirect heating, for example from the heat given off by underfloor heating. This technology could also be beneficial in swimming pools and
bathrooms.

Further interesting possibilities are opening up for the use of *Chronos Chro-
mos Concrete* with the thermal energy given off in rooms. For example, as
suggested by Glaister, Mehin and Rosen, the trafficked floor surfaces in the
Tate Gallery, London, could be formed in concrete that would display partial
colour changes produced by the heat given off by people standing and moving on them. Spots of intense colour, or lines of less intense colour, would
be produced in response to the heat given off by people, standing or in mo-
tion, whenever the difference between the room temperature and the surface
temperatures of the people in the room was large enough.

The students' first proposed application was for oversized digital clocks integrated into walls and balustrades.

Simulations: a digital clock integrated into a balustrade at the Tate Gallery. | A
digital clock integrated into a wall. | Thermopool. | Partial colouring of the floor of
the Tate Gallery triggered by human body heat.

ELECTROCHROMIC AND ELECTROOPTIC
SMART MATERIALS >
MATERIALS, PRODUCTS, PROJECTS

Their inherent properties enable them to react to electrical fields by reversibly changing their colour and/or their optical characteristics.

The following electrochromic and electrooptic smart materials are currently of interest to architects:

ELECTROCHROMIC MATERIALS (EC)

ELECTROOPTIC MATERIALS (EO)

These materials and products include:

ELECTROOPTIC GLASS SYSTEMS INCORPORATING POLYMER-DISPERSED LIQUID CRYSTALS (PDLC)

ELECTROOPTIC GLASS SYSTEMS INCORPORATING SUSPENDED PARTICLE DEVICES (SPD)

ELECTROCHROMIC GLASS SYSTEMS INCORPORATING METAL OXIDES

Systems incorporating suspended particle devices (SPD) will not be dealt with in more detail here.

electrochromic/-optic materials (EC, EO) › materials

Electrochromic materials (EC) and electrochromics are materials or components that are able to reversibly change their colour in response to light. In contrast to this, electrooptic materials (EO) are materials or components that are able to reversibly change their optical characteristics (e.g. transparency) in response to temperature.

Electrochemical cells are required in order to use the phenomenon of electrochromism. These cells can be differentiated according to their four basic types. They differ from each other in their number of combined electrochemical switchable films, among other properties.

At the moment type 1 is the most popular. This type has two films of different electrochromic components combined with one another. In principle, type 1 consists of several functional layers placed one upon the other as follows: a transparent conductive layer (TCO), commonly indium tin oxide (ITO), is deposited as an anode on a supporting first substrate layer such as glass. On top of this is placed the first anodic electrochromic layer of e.g. tungsten oxide (WO_3), which is responsible for the colour change. It can be applied by vacuum technology (vapour deposition, sputtering), Sol-Gel technology or electrochemically. Then follows an electrolytic layer of e.g. a polymer electrolyte, which should be as good as possible at conducting ions but at the same time be a poor electrical conductor. The rest of the construction is the reverse of the above. Another metal oxide such as niobium oxide (Nb_2O_5) or a conductive polymer such as polyaniline can be used as the second cathodic electrochromic layer.

EOs include liquid crystals that have been processed into films in order that they can be used as electrooptic layers. Liquid crystal films (LC films) in principle consist of several functional layers: two PET substrate layers, which are coated on the inner sides with a transparent conductive oxide (TCO), e.g. indium tin oxide (ITO), to serve as electrodes, enclose a polymer matrix in which the liquid crystals are embedded. These liquid crystals are also known as polymer-dispersed liquid crystals (PDLC).

Electrochromism became known in 1953 following the work of Kraus on tungsten trioxide, which he found changed colour to deep blue after the application of an electric field. In 1969 and 1973 S.K. Deb published his research work on thin films of molybdenum and tungsten trioxide, which established the principles of modern electrochromism. In the 1970s Nick Sheridon, a researcher at Xerox Parc, developed the first electronic paper (e-paper). On the European market the first commercial electrooptic glass was introduced under the brand name PRIVA-LITE in 1991. This system is still available today and is based on liquid crystals. It switches reversibly between transparent and opaque.

In 2004, American researchers working with Fred Wudl at the University of California made public their development of a green electrochromic polymer which together with the already available red and blue electrochromic polymers enables any other colour to be created. Also in 2004, as well as a photochromic system, a photo-electrochromic system consisting of a combination of a dye solar cell with an electrochromic cell was developed in Germany at the Fraunhofer Institute for Solar Energy Systems, Freiburg.

EC materials and components generally used include among others:

ORGANIC COMPOUNDS
Cathodic colouring viologenes (bipyridinium salts)
Anodic colouring polymers (e.g. polypyrrol, polyaniline, polythiophene derivates)
Cathodic colouring polymers (e.g. polythiophene derivates)

INORGANIC COMPOUNDS
Cathodic colouring metal oxides (e.g. tungsten oxide (WO_3), molybdenum oxide (MoO_3), niobium oxide (Nb_2O_5))
Anodic colouring metal oxides, other metal compounds (e.g. nickel oxide (NiO), iridium oxide (IrO_2), ferric hexacyanoferrate (Prussian blue))

EO materials and components generally used include among others:

ORGANIC COMPOUNDS
Liquid crystals (stilbene derivates)

The following ECs and EOs could be among those of interest in architecture:

POLYANILINE DERIVATES
Electrically conductive polymers that can be made by the electrochemical polymerisation of aniline (derivates). Solid at +20°C. Can be used e.g. as anodic colouring compounds in electrochromic layers (films). They react to the influence of a DC electrical field by electrochemical oxidation with the simultaneous taking-in of charge-neutralising cations (e.g. H+, Li+), changing colour from transparent through green to violet. Reversing the polarity reverses the colour change. Aniline is available as a liquid.
➕ Market presence, can be made in large quantities, can be used in low to high temperatures (< –40°C to > +120°C), relatively large number of cycles of possible changes of colour (> 105), reversibly colouring between three oxidation stages, non-toxic.
➖ Cannot form neutral colours (green and violet are considered less suitable for some applications), relatively poor lightfastness compared with inorganic electrochromic compounds based on metal oxides.

POLYTHIOPHENE DERIVATES

Electrically conductive polymers that can be made by the electrochemical polymerisation of thiophene (derivates). Solid at +20°C. They can be used e.g. as cathodic colouring compounds in electrochromic layers (films). React to the influence of a DC electrical field by electrochemical reduction with the simultaneous taking-in of charge-neutralising cations (e.g. H+, Li+), changing colour from red to blue. Other colours are possible depending on the derivate. Reversing the polarity reverses the colour change. Thiophene is available in powder form.

+ Market presence, can be made in large quantities, can be used in low to high temperatures (< –40°C to > +120°C), relatively large number of cycles of possible changes of colour (> 105), non-toxic.

– Only reversibly colouring between two oxidation stages, cannot form neutral colours (red and blue are considered less suitable for some applications), relatively poor lightfastness compared with inorganic electrochromic compounds based on metal oxides.

TUNGSTEN OXIDE (WO$_3$)

A metal oxide that can be made by the oxidation of the heavy metal tungsten with pure oxygen and by heating tungstic acid. Solid at +20°C. It can be used e.g. as cathodic colouring compound in electrochromic layers (films). It reacts to the influence of a DC electrical field by electrochemical reduction with the simultaneous taking-in of charge-neutralising cations (e.g. H+, Li+), changing colour from transparent to blue. Reversing the polarity reverses the colour change. Available as a yellow powder.

+ Market presence, can be made in large quantities, even by the user himself, can be used in low to high temperatures (< -40°C to > +120°C), relatively large number of possible cycles of colour change (> 105), relatively good lightfastness compared with organic electrochromic compounds based on polymers, non-toxic.

– Only reversibly colouring between two oxidation stages, cannot form neutral colours (blue is considered less suitable for some applications).

NIOBIUM OXIDE (NB$_2$O$_5$)

A metal oxide that can be made by the oxidation of the heavy metal niobium with pure oxygen. Solid at +20°C. Reacts by changing from transparent to brown. Available as a powder. Is being currently tried as a replacement for tungsten oxide. Otherwise as above.

+ Can form a neutral colour (brown). Otherwise as above.

– Only reversibly colouring between two oxidation stages. Otherwise as above.

STILBENE-DERIVATES (C$_{14}$H$_{12}$)

Aromatic hydrocarbons with the isomer forms cis- and trans-stilbenes.

+ Market presence, can be used in low to high temperatures (< –20°C to > +100°C).

– Not known.

Tungsten oxide (WO$_3$) |
Prussian blue.

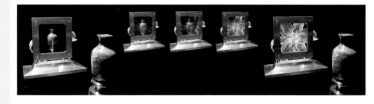

Technology by Gesimat: two mounted glass panels with tungsten oxide as the cathodic colouring electrochromic layer in combination with Prussian blue as the anodic colouring electrochromic layer, left glass in the decoloured state, right glass in the coloured state. | Technology by LBL: technology demonstrator of a smart window with an electrically switchable mirror (TMSM); bottom half reflective, top half transparent. | Smart window in different reflective and transparent states. | Technology by Gesimat: electrochromic glass system.

electrochromic/-optic materials (ec, eo) › products

In contrast to electrochromic materials (EC), electrooptic materials (EO) have performed relatively well on the market. Liquid crystals are found today in displays, e.g. in televisions, as well as in electrochromic layers in glass systems.

ECs were first tried in displays. As liquid crystals eventually emerged as the more suitable materials, efforts are now concentrated on electrically switchable filters and mirrors, e.g. for active solar protection of rooms, antidazzle layers in automobile mirrors and as electronic inks (e inks), e.g. as displays in e-books, so-called electronic paper (e paper).

The following products made from or incorporating ECs and EOs are of particular interest for architectural applications:

Transparent layers with electrochromic organic or inorganic compounds:

GLASS SYSTEM INCORPORATING EC (TECHNOLOGY BY GESIMAT)
Type 1 electrochemical cells consisting of two different electrochromic layers of cathodic and anodic colouring compounds (e.g. tungsten oxide with Prussian blue), joined together with a polymer electrolyte layer and enclosed between electrically conductive glass substrates (2 mm x 4 mm or 2 mm x 6 mm). Depending on the colouring compounds used, after the application of a DC electrical field two filters with different transmission colours that absorb different radiation spectra of natural light are created, and by interaction they determine the overall colour effect of the system. Reversing the polarity reverses the colour change. The colour depth and transparency and therefore the absorption capacity can be controlled electrically. The glass system provides active solar protection of rooms and can be used like conventional glass systems. The maximum dimensions of the currently manufactured panels (technology demonstrators) are 120 cm x 80 cm. Current products are about to enter the pilot production stage.
+ Can be used in low to medium temperatures (< –20°C to > +80°C), medium to long replacement life (approx. 200 000 switching cycles, small formats), requires a relatively low switching voltage (< 5 V DC), a permanently applied electrical field is not required for the transparent state, suitable for room darkening (light transmittance in the off state approx. 75 %, in the on state approx. 8 %), largely lightfast, can be used adjacent to conventional glass construction, therefore allowing clean detailing, relatively easy to use, adequate fire resistance, relatively inexpensive to manufacture compared with glass systems based on liquid crystals. Otherwise as for tungsten oxide, Prussian blue above.
– Lack of market presence, can be made only in small quantities, higher costs of replacement, e.g. of damaged panes, relatively heavy, with resulting higher installation costs, electrochromic coating of the edges of the cells is not possible, hence edge covering is necessary. Otherwise as for tungsten oxide, Prussian blue above.

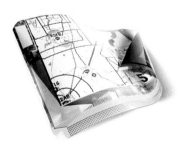

Technology by E INK and others: technology demonstrator of a flexible digital clock (Citizen). | Technology demonstrators of flexible E INK paper displays (LG.Philips LCD, Polymer Vision).

NON-FLEXIBLE AND FLEXIBLE DISPLAYS INCORPORATING EC (TECHNOLOGY BY E INK AND OTHERS)

These consist of capsules of black and white pigment chips suspended in a clear liquid enclosed between two electrically conductive substrates (e.g. polyethylenterephthalate (PET), glass). The individual capsules are electrically controllable. The distribution of pigment changes in response to the polarity of the DC electrical field on each side of a capsule, which, in combination with other capsules, produces the overall colour of the system. Reversing the polarity reverses the colour change. The system is used to display graphics and alphanumeric characters and can, with limitations, be used like conventional displays. Currently they are in the market introduction phase.

+ Can be used in low to medium temperatures (< –10°C to > +60°C, depending on components), medium to long replacement life (approx. 200 000 switching cycles, depending on the system, among other parameters), requires a relatively low switching voltage (< 50 V DC, depending on the system, among other parameters), a permanently applied electrical field is not required to maintain any state.

– Little market presence.

Transparent layers incorporating electrooptic organic compounds:

GLASS SYSTEM INCORPORATING EO (PRIVA-LITE, TECHNOLOGY BY SGG)

Basic type (laminated glass) consisting of two laminated films between glass substrates (2 mm x 5 mm), which are joined to one another by an electrooptic film of liquid crystals in a polymer matrix with electrically conductive coatings (ITO) on both sides. Upon the application of an AC electrical field, the previously transparent layer becomes translucent (milky white turbidity) due to the irregular orientation of the crystals within the liquid crystal layer, which can then reflect or absorb different spectra of natural light. The crystals assume their regular orientation and the turbidity clears when the polarity is reversed. Transparency and the amount of absorption and reflection can be set electrically. The glass system provides active privacy or a projection surface and can be used like conventional glass systems.
The maximum available dimension of a panel is 300 cm x 100 cm.

+ Market presence, can be made in large quantities, can be used in low to medium temperatures (–20°C to +60°C), long replacement life (over 15 years in use), can be used adjacent to conventional glass construction, therefore allowing clean detailing, relatively easy to use, adequate fire resistance. Otherwise as for liquid crystals above.

– Relatively high switching voltage required (100 V AC, Europe), a permanently connected electrical field is required for the transparent state, not suitable for darkening rooms (light transmittance in the off state approx. 76%), higher costs of replacement, e.g. of damaged panes, relatively heavy, with resulting higher installation costs, electrooptic coating of the edges of the cells is not possible, hence edge covering is necessary, expensive to manufacture and install (currently approx. 1700 euro/m^2 to 2000 euro/m^2, supplied and installed). Otherwise as for liquid crystals above.

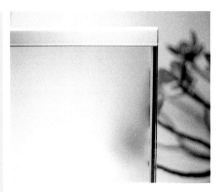

The requirements for handling and processing the products depend on the technology and the EC or EO used. With all glass- and plastic-laminated transparent systems, the substrate must not be overstressed, e.g. by compression, which may arise from inadequately specified installation tolerances. Moisture must also not be allowed to penetrate the electrical connections. Some electrochromic and electrooptic glasses are not suitable for installation as overhead roof lights. In addition, the specified voltages must not be exceeded.

Products currently used in architecture include:

RAW OR END PRODUCTS:

DYES incorporating ECs (technology by E INK)

FILMS incorporating ECs (technology by E INK)

FILMS incorporating ECs (technology by Gesimat)

FILMS incorporating EOs (PRIVA-LITE, technology by SGG)

INTERMEDIATE OR END PRODUCTS:

GLASS SYSTEM incorporating ECs (technology by Gesimat)

GLASS SYSTEM (mirrors) incorporating ECs (TMSM, technology by LBL)

POLYMER SYSTEM incorporating ECs (technology by E INK)

GLASS SYSTEM incorporating EOs (PRIVA-LITE, technology by SGG).

electrochromic/-optic materials (EC, EO) › projects

There are only a few companies in the world that can manufacture electrochromic glass. Two German companies are FLABEG and Gesimat. Unlike the situation with electrooptic systems, so far there have been only a few completed applications of electrochromic systems in Europe, mainly because Gesimat and other companies do not yet have an electrochromic system in series production.

One completed application was an accessible glass roof over the main reading room of the Landesbibliothek Dresden, Germany (1996 to 2002), which was designed by the S.L.U.B. joint venture and fitted with electrochromic glazing supplied by FLABEG. This glazing was later replaced by conventional glazing.

The following example shows that electrochromic glazing can also be used in old buildings. Here two switchable panes were fitted with the help of putty into the external window frames of a conventional wooden box window. The objective was to test the long-term behaviour of the glass under real operating conditions.

Electrooptic switchable systems are currently becoming more popular worldwide, in particular the PRIVA-LITE product manufactured by Saint Gobain Glass (SGG). Apart from dividing walls, doors etc. that have been manufactured and installed to provide temporary optical separation to parts of rooms, the world's largest contiguous switchable electrooptical surface to date was built into a facade in Tokyo in 2004.

Technology by Gesimat: a two-casement box window with electrochromic glazing. | Separating wall with electrooptic glass (PRIVA-LITE): *Burnett* (SGG). | Informational display at the EXPO 2005 in Japan (E INK, TOPPAN-KANBAN). | *opposite:* Technology by SGG: electrooptic glass system, in translucent and transparent states.

chanel Ginza

Monosmart material | Polysmart application
Colour- and optically changing smart material:
ELECTROOPTIC GLASS
Light-emitting smart material:
LIGHT EMITTING DIODES (LED)
Communication and advertising with electrooptic glass

Peter Marino Associates, USA
High rise facade | Tokyo, Japan (2004)

A new headquarters for the fashion group Chanel was completed in 2004 in the Tokyo district of Ginza. The ten-storey highrise contains a 1300 m² shopping centre, a concert hall and a restaurant.

Its 910 m² display facade, which allows the 56 m high building to take on different appearances throughout the day, is currently the only one of its type in the world. It consists of a laminate with several functional layers. The outer curtain wall is formed of grey glass, which, in conjunction with the directly adjacent stainless steel, rhombic-honeycombed structure, gives the building an elegant appearance, reminiscent of Chanel's signature tweed pattern. Next follows a gap and an electrooptic switchable layer of PRIVA-LITE. The internal face is formed from a two-pane laminated safety glass interrupted by horizontally running aluminium rails in which a double row of white LEDs are integrated.

By day the electrooptic glass and hence the whole facade is switched to the transparent state. The view into the building is unobstructed. By night the glass is switched to opaque and the facade provides a projection surface for the 700000 LEDs, which are controlled by three main control computers and 65000 microcomputers capable of processing a total of over 32 trillion commands per second.

The display facade can show still images as well as video presentations.

Chanel Ginza: facade at night in an animated state. |
General view.

Chanel Ginza: simulation of possible effects. |
Trial construction from inside.

adhesion-changing smart materials

Adhesion-changing smart materials include materials and products that are able to change reversibly the attraction forces of adsorption or absorption of an atom or molecule of a solid, liquid or gaseous component in response to a stimulus. This may take place due to the effect of light, temperature, an electrical field or a liquid and/or biological component.

Whilst adhesion describes the attraction forces between atoms and molecules of different components, cohesion is the attraction of forces between atoms and molecules of the same component.

Adsorption is the attachment of an atom or molecule of a component to an inner surface of a material or product, the adsorbent. Absorption describes an inclusion of an atom or molecule of a component into the free volume of a material and/or product, the absorbent. The release of a previously adsorbed or absorbed atom or molecule is termed desorption (see matter-exchanging smart materials, p. 174).

The processes can be generally differentiated as:

PHYSICAL ADHESION
The main attraction forces are due to adsorption, secondary bonding, van-der-Waals forces, electrostatic bonding, dipolar bonding and secondary valency bonding between different components.
CHEMICAL ADHESION
Chemical bonding provides the main attraction forces between different components.
MECHANICAL ADHESION
These attraction forces arise mainly from interlocking, anchoring or intermeshing between different components.

Depending on the stimulus involved adhesion-changing smart materials can be differentiated as:

PHOTOADHESIVE SMART MATERIALS
Change the attraction forces of adsorption or absorption of atoms or molecules of solid, liquid or gaseous components in response to light.
THERMOADHESIVE SMART MATERIALS
Change the attraction forces of adsorption or absorption of atoms or molecules of solid, liquid or gaseous components in response to temperature.

Example of adhesion on a hibiscus flower.

ELECTROADHESIVE SMART MATERIALS
Change the attraction forces of adsorption or absorption of atoms or molecules of solid, liquid or gaseous components in response to an electrical field.
HYDROADHESIVE SMART MATERIALS
Change the attraction forces of adsorption or absorption of atoms or molecules of solid, liquid or gaseous components in response to liquid components (e.g. water).
BIOADHESIVE SMART MATERIALS
Change the attraction forces of adsorption or absorption of atoms or molecules of solid, liquid or gaseous components in response to biological components (e.g. bacteria).

Thermoplastic plastics are one example of smart materials that have strong thermoadhesive properties. They create a temperature-dependent bond between different components. Electroadhesive smart materials are able to generate an electrostatic field in response to a stimulus and reversibly bond with ionised particles floating in the air, to give an example. Bioadhesive smart materials can be considered to include living bacteria on a nutrient and carrier layer (e.g. agar), which secrete adhesive substances, e.g. in the form of polysaccharide fibres in response to light or nutrients.

Currently, photo- and hydroadhesive smart materials are of particular relevance in the field of architecture. Photoadhesive smart materials change e.g. the wetting angle of liquid components applied to solid components in response to light. Hydroadhesive smart materials include materials that generate water in response to light by electrical conversion; the water might act as the adhesive medium between two solid components. One publication describes a gripping mechanism, functioning by hydroadhesion, which is cooled electrically by a Peltier element (PE) to such an extent that it freezes to form a firm bond on contact with water-soaked textiles (see [9]). The use of PEs in architecture will be dealt with in greater detail elsewhere (see thermoelectric generators (TEG), pp. 148 ff.).

Monte Verde: self-cleaning facade with TiO$_2$. | *Garden Chapel:* self-cleaning construction membrane with TiO$_2$.

PHOTOADHESIVE SMART MATERIALS >
MATERIALS, PRODUCTS, PROJECTS

Their inherent properties allow products based on photoadhesive materials to change reversibly their adhesion in response to light.

In architecture the following photoadhesive material and products manufactured from it are of interest:

TITANIUM DIOXIDE (TiO$_2$)

titanium dioxide (TiO$_2$) › materials

Titanium dioxide (TiO$_2$) is currently the most technically important compound of titanium. It occurs naturally as the crystal lattice structures (also described as modifications) rutile, anatase and brookite. Raw materials for production are a titanium iron ore by the name of ilmenite, a shiny black mineral, and rutile, a less iron-rich titanium ore; both of these are obtained from opencast mines. TiO$_2$ is insoluble in water, organic solvents, diluted acids and alkalis. It is lightfast and temperature-stable (its melting point is at 1855°C).

TiO$_2$ was first used as a white pigment. It was made in the USA and sold from 1909 under the name Kronos titanium white. In Germany, it was manufactured from 1924 as Degea-Titanweiß, at first as the anatase modification and then from 1938 in the rutile form. Since 1917, TiO$_2$ has been produced from ilmenite (titanium iron ore) using the sulphate process by the addition of sulphuric acid. From 1958 also the chloride process has been in use. Here chlorine is added to the ore. Since 1968, TiO$_2$ has also been used as a foodstuff additive. After its photocatalytic effect had been discovered, the Japanese were successful in 1995 in using TiO$_2$ in ceramic surface coatings. In recent years Japan also developed paper and building membranes with photocatalytic effects. 2002 saw the first self-cleaning glass with TiO$_2$ appear on the European market.

Materials and components in use include:

MODIFICATIONS
Rutile, anatase

Both modifications are of interest in architecture:

RUTILE
+ Market presence, can be made in large quantities, usable over a comparatively large temperature range (< –10°C to > +80°C), depending on the applied source material), used in particular as a white pigment and as a photocatalyst for converting pollutants and for creating a hydrophilic effect, better covering properties compared with the anatase modification, non-consumptive, non-toxic.
– Not available everywhere, effects are light-dependent, only about 5% of the solar radiation (absorption of radiation < 413 nm wavelength) can be used.

ANATASE MODIFICATION (TETRAGONAL TiO$_2$ CRYSTALS)
+ Used as a white pigment, in particular as a photocatalyst for converting organic pollutants and for creating a hydrophilic effect. Otherwise as above.
– Only about 5% of the solar radiation (absorption of radiation < 388 nm wavelength) can be used. Otherwise as above.

TiO$_2$ powder.

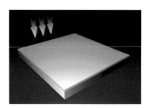

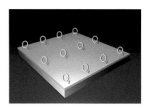
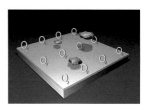

titanium dioxide (tio₂) › products

One of the successful areas of application of titanium dioxide (TiO₂), especially in Japan and also in Germany, is in photocatalytic paper, which uses the UV light to oxidise organic molecule pollutants and odours in the air and convert them into substances such as carbon dioxide and water. The cellulose in the paper is hygroscopic and adsorbs water vapour; therefore the product has no significant self-cleaning properties. Photocatalytic papers are expected to be further developed for the European market, for example as wallpaper. In Japan it has occasionally been incorporated in coverings for room dividers for domestic use.

TiO₂ can also be used, with the help of sunlight, to purify water, e.g. breaking down pesticides and pharmaceutical residues. In the 1970s American scientist A. Heller and Japanese scientists A. Fujishima and K. Honda described the photocatalytic process as follows: "When UV light strikes the surface of the TiO₂ anatase crystal, it releases negatively charged electrons from the surface leaving behind positively charged holes. In the presence of water, OH-groups are adsorbed on the TiO₂ surface. The bond is so strong that further layers of H₂O on the monomolecular OH-layer are physically adsorbed and other substances repelled from the surface, creating an easy-to-clean, hydrophilic surface. Water droplets immediately spread on the hydrophilic surface and form a compact film with the result that the contact angle is very low." (after [10])

Various products with surfaces made of TiO₂ and capable of changing reversibly their adhesion in response to UV light have been developed for architectural applications. The most important products developed over recent years are those in which the anatase modification has been applied insolubly using the Sol-Gel process, preferably on to smooth surfaces. The first marketable product was developed in Japan in the form of ceramic slabs which had self-cleaning properties and were able to break down pollutant gases. From this have followed construction membranes, glass panes and other products for various applications. In addition there are various products on the market that use TiO₂ solely for breaking down organic pollutants. By the choice of components used the products have no overall light-dependent hydrophilic properties but show a permanent hydrophobic effect. Silicones are used to achieve this effect in certain photocatalytic facade paints. Further similar products with a photocatalytic effect are interior paints and plasters.

Illustration of the self-cleaning effect. | Illustration of the photocatalytic conversion of organic pollutants.

Below are described some products specifically developed for architectural uses and equipped with the ability to change reversibly their adhesion in response to UV light:

CERAMIC SLABS WITH TiO$_2$
Ceramic slabs with a surface coating of baked-on TiO$_2$, preferably the anatase modification, currently available as facade slabs (e.g. with dimensions 592 mm x 284 mm x 15 mm) and as wall and floor tiles, can be handled and used like conventional facade slabs and tiles. They are intended for use where their self-cleaning properties and their ability to improve the air quality by breaking down organic pollutants are important.
+ Market presence, can be made in large quantities, applicable in conjunction with conventional facade substructures, largely maintenance-free, long replacement life, fire-resistant, relatively inexpensive compared with conventional ceramic slabs. Otherwise as above for the anatase modification.
− Only a few manufacturers, reactivation by additional cleaning is required where there is severe dirt contamination (e.g. bird droppings, tar). Otherwise as above for the anatase modification.

CONSTRUCTION MEMBRANES WITH TiO$_2$
Textile membranes fully coated with plastic (e.g. PVC, PTFE) with a TiO$_2$ surface coating, preferably the anatase modification. Available in rolls in various dimensions depending on the manufacturer, extensive cutting to shape required, can be prefabricated to suit the customer's requirements as conventional construction membranes, best suited for use where self-cleaning is desirable (no knowledge of its suitability for air quality improvement by breaking down organic pollutants; the release of volatile components from the plastic shortly after installation and at high temperatures may present problems).
+ Market presence, can be made in large quantities, can be used for a wide range of applications and integrated into various membrane construction types, largely mainte-nance-free, long replacement life. Otherwise as above for the anatase modification.
− Only a few manufacturers, reactivation by additional cleaning is required where there is severe dirt contamination (e.g. bird droppings, tar), may have a plastic odour, possible release of toxic components in the event of fire. Otherwise as above for the anatase modification.

Ceramic facade slabs with TiO$_2$. | Ceramic wall and floor tiles with TiO$_2$. | *opposite:* Illustration showing the self-cleaning effect: without TiO$_2$. | Photocatalysis with UV light and TiO$_2$. | Subsequent hydrophilic effect.

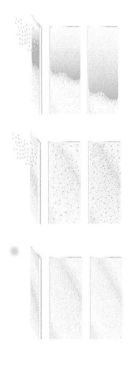

GLASS PANES WITH TiO$_2$

Conventional glass panes with a TiO$_2$ surface coating, preferably the anatase modification. Available as flat glass in various sizes depending on the manufacturer, extensive cutting to shape required. They can be prefabricated to suit the customer's requirements as conventional glass panes. They are best suited for use where self-cleaning and air quality improvement by breaking down organic pollutants is desirable.

+ Market presence, can be made in large quantities, can be used for a wide range of applications and integrated into framed and frameless construction types, largely maintenance-free, long replacement life. Otherwise as above for the anatase modification.

– Reactivation by additional cleaning is required where there is severe dirt contamination (e.g. bird droppings, tar). Otherwise as above for the anatase modification.

Available or developed products useful in architecture include:

RAW OR END PRODUCTS:

FINE GRANULATE (powder) TiO$_2$
(e.g. anatase modification)

PAINTS containing TiO$_2$ (e.g. rutile modification, not adhesion-changing)

INTERMEDIATE OR END PRODUCTS:

PAPER containing TiO$_2$ (not adhesion-changing)

CERAMIC SLABS with TiO$_2$

CONSTRUCTION MEMBRANES with TiO$_2$

GLASS PANES with TiO$_2$

Technology by Deutsche Steinzeug: ceramic slabs with TiO_2. | Technology by Taiyo: various construction membranes with TiO_2. | Technology by Pilkington: glass construction with TiO_2.

titanium dioxide (TiO_2) › projects

Products incorporating titanium dioxide (TiO_2) with the properties detailed above have become well established worldwide and particularly in Japanese, European and US-American markets. Licences for the use of the technology mainly based on the patents of US and Japanese companies have been granted to several manufacturers.

Following the successful construction in Japan of the first building with facade slabs incorporating TiO_2, facades are now appearing in Europe with photocatalytic, self-cleaning properties. The main country where construction membranes containing TiO_2 are used is still Japan, the home of the system developer Taiyo Kogyo Corporation, who has limited the award of licences to several companies in Japan as well as in China, Taiwan and Thailand. The acquisition of a traditional German company means that self-cleaning membranes and textile structures can be expected to become more common in Europe as well.

Since its introduction in Europe in 2002 all well-known major manufacturers now offer a self-cleaning glass product. As the additional cost is small compared to conventional float glass, it has already been used in projects by private and public clients. In addition to smaller areas on buildings, the technology has been used on comparatively large complex areas of glass to reduce running costs by dispensing with time- and cost-intensive cleaning routines and permanently installed cleaning platforms, and to give the building an uncluttered appearance, clear of distracting attachments.

garden chapel

Monosmart material | Monosmart application
Adhesion-changing smart materials:
CONSTRUCTION MEMBRANE WITH TiO₂
Self-cleaning surfaces

Obayashi Corporation, Japan
Chapel with photocatalytic, self-cleaning membrane skin |
Hyatt Regency Hotel, Osaka, Japan (2001)

Membranes can be formed into technically and geometrically complex textile structures which can possess a special aesthetic charm. The earlier disadvantage was that if maintenance was neglected or cleaning was not carried out or was inadequate then the membranes would become unsightly after a few years.

In January 2001 in the garden of a luxury hotel in Osaka, Japan, a chapel was built which incorporates a white construction membrane. The surface that is exposed to rain was given a self-cleaning coating containing TiO₂. The double-curved, load-bearing structure of the chapel is open on two sides and has four supports. It is clad externally with numerous rows of tied filigree rhomboids on which about 50m² of the membrane were applied.

The shape, surface texture and permanent self-cleaning white colour of the structure suggest a lightweight bridal gown moving in the wind.

Garden Chapel: night view and daylight view.

monte verde

Monosmart material | Monosmart application
Adhesion-changing smart materials:
CONSTRUCTION MEMBRANE WITH TiO₂
Self-cleaning surfaces

Albert Wimmer, AN_architects, Austria
High-rise with photocatalytic self-cleaning
ceramic facade | Vienna, Austria (2004)

Wienerberg City, a new district in south Vienna, is the location for architect Albert Wimmer's 77 m high, green, glistening apartment tower Monte Verde for which AN_architects were engaged to design the photocatalytic facade.

The 182 apartment building is in the shape of a flat cuboid standing on its end, with additional smaller cuboids individually superimposed upon its surface. While the narrow ends of the tower in the north and south have conventional facades, the sides with the superimposed parallelepipeds facing west and east have a self-cleaning photocatalytic facade system.

The ceramic facade slabs used here have a specially designed, blue-green glaze on which the titanium oxide-containing "Hydrotect" surface coating was applied by spray as a transparent liquid and then baked on.

In correspondence with the characteristics of the coating, the facade is able to use light to form a hydrophilic surface on which the water drops striking it form a compact film due to their reduced contact angle. Any dirt particles, e.g. rust or dust, deposited out of air are more easily washed off along with the rainwater drops flowing off the surface.

In addition to the self-cleaning effect there is also a light-responsive air cleaning effect due to activated oxygen, which is generated by the free electrons formed at the surface of the coating.

Scientific tests have shown that 1000 m² of photocatalytic-coated facade surface achieved an air cleaning effect that was the equivalent of 70 medium-sized deciduous trees. Pro-rata the 6800 m² ceramic facade of the Monte Verde would be the equivalent of 476 similar trees, put aside its additional qualities and functions such as the oxygen production. For some cities with severe air pollution, photocatalytic ceramic facades would help to ensure that air pollution does not increase, assuming that enough natural light of the correct wavelength range strikes the facades.

Monte Verde: general view. | Sections of photocatalytic facade.

Monte Verde: facade section.

energy-exchanging smart materials

light-emitting smart materials

Light-emitting smart materials include materials or products with molecules that become excited by the effect of energy, e.g. the effects of light or an electrical field, to emit light. This happens as a result of the molecules taking up a temporary state of higher energy before leaving it again, at which time part of the energy taken up is emitted in the form of visible electromagnetic radiation, without the simultaneous emission of considerable thermal radiation. This optical phenomenon is called luminescence.

In contrast, there are also materials or products with molecules that become excited by the effect of energy, for instance the direct or indirect application of heat, and emit heat as well as light. These molecules take up a temporary higher energy state and emit visible electromagnetic radiation, but the larger part of the energy emitted is thermal radiation. These materials are not considered as smart materials and are not dealt with further in this book.

In general terms luminescence can be differentiated as:

PHOTOLUMINESCENCE
An optical phenomenon in which a molecule is excited and emits light due to the effect of light.
ELECTROLUMINESCENCE
An optical phenomenon in which a molecule is excited and emits light due to the effect of an electrical field.
BIOLUMINESCENCE
An optical phenomenon in which a chemical reaction occurs to excite a molecule in a living organism to emit light.
CHEMOLUMINESCENCE
An optical phenomenon in which a chemical reaction occurs to excite a molecule to emit light.
CRYSTALLOLUMINESCENCE
An optical phenomenon in which a molecule is excited due to crystallisation and emits light.
RADIOLUMINESCENCE
An optical phenomenon in which a molecule is excited by the effect of radioactive radiation and emits light.
RADIOPHOTOLUMINESCENCE (THERMOLUMINESCENCE)
An optical phenomenon in which a molecule is excited by the effect of radioactive radiation followed by thermal radiation to emit cold light.
TRIBOLUMINESCENCE
An optical phenomenon in which a molecule is excited by a mechanical effect to emit light.

Currently, the most important architectural applications are photoluminescence and electroluminescence. In the near future bioluminescence and triboluminescence will be among those gaining in importance.

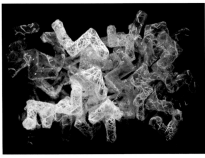

Leuchtzimmer: paper with fluorescent paint. |
Lost Embryo: threads with flourescent pigments.

PHOTOLUMINESCENT SMART MATERIALS >
MATERIALS, PRODUCTS, PROJECTS

Photoluminescent materials and products can be classed as fluorescent or phosphorescent depending on the properties of their luminous behaviour with respect to time.

FLUORESCENCE
The excitement of a molecule by light, in particular by its ultraviolet radiation component; the transition from the excited state back to the ground state is accompanied by almost simultaneous light emission.

PHOSPHORESCENCE
The excitement of a molecule by light radiation; the transition from the excited state back to the ground state is accompanied by delayed light emission.

Solid organic daylight-luminous pigments. |
Daylight-luminous pigment from fluorescene.

fluorescence › materials

Materials or components with a reversible capability for fluorescence are capable, by absorption of electromagnetic radiation in the form of light, of emitting light almost exactly on transition from the excited singlet state back to the ground state, within a period not greater than 10^{-8} seconds [11].

Depending on the usable light spectrum or on the particular application, fluorescent materials or components can be further divided into:

DAYLIGHT-LUMINOUS MATERIALS OR COMPONENTS

These materials emit light during the day by absorbing the invisible ultraviolet component of daylight and emitting light almost simultaneously. This effect is particularly clear under overcast skies or at dusk. The effect can be increased if an artificial ultraviolet light source is used, particularly in darkened rooms.

Some materials or components that are daylight-luminous include:

ORGANIC MATERIALS

Fluorescene, rhodamine, cyclam, perylene.

UV-LUMINOUS MATERIALS OR COMPONENTS

These materials emit light only when they are exposed to an artificial ultraviolet radiation source.

Materials or components that are UV-luminous include:

INORGANIC MATERIALS

Zinc sulphide cadmium sulphide mixed crystals.

PHOSPHORESCENT MATERIALS OR COMPONENTS

These materials are used for example in fluorescent tubes; they convert the ultraviolet light generated there into white light

Materials or components used as phosphors include:

INORGANIC MATERIALS

Rare earths (e.g. yttrium oxide)

Fluorescent materials or components include:

MINERALS
Scheelite (blue, yellow luminescence), sodalite, calcite (orange-red luminescence), halite.

The materials of most interest to the field of architecture are:

FLUORESCENE, RHODAMINE, CYCLAM, PERYLENE
Organic materials for the manufacture of daylight-luminous pigments.
+ Market presence, can be made in large quantities, wide choice of colours, many years of practical use, high brilliance and intensity of colour, free of heavy metals, non-toxic, versatile range of applications; depending on type, resistance to particular chemicals and high temperatures, also available in small quantities, inexpensive.
– Limited lightfastness.

fluorescence › products

A long-term market presence means that raw, semifinished and end products have been developed and made commercially available for a wide range of applications. They extend from pigments and paints through composite materials with e.g. paper to carpets and complex plastic housings.

In architecture there is particular interest in the following products involving daylight-luminous organic pigments and UV-luminous inorganic pigments, some of which can be applied directly to walls, for example, or processed into further products:

Paints containing daylight-luminous organic pigments:

DAYLIGHT-LUMINOUS DISPERSION-BASED PAINTS
They can be applied by brush, roller or spray to surfaces such as wood, plastic, textiles, paper, cardboard, concrete and masonry.
+ High flexibility, good adhesion.
– Limited lightfastness.

DAYLIGHT-LUMINOUS PAINTS BASED ON TWO-COMPONENT ACRYLATE-BASED PAINT
They can be applied by brush, roller or spray to surfaces such as metal, wood and glass.
+ Good resistance to mechanical loads, good adhesion, highly dirt-repellent, simple to clean, resistance to wear with additional protective coating.
– Limited lightfastness

Daylight-luminous paint based on two-component acrylate-based paint system. | *opposite:* Polyacryl-based granulate.

Currently available or developed products
useful in architecture include:

RAW OR END PRODUCTS

ORGANIC PIGMENTS e.g. fluorescene

INORGANIC PIGMENTS e.g. zinc sulphide
cadmium sulphide mixed crystals

PAINTS containing luminous organic pigments

PAINTS containing fluorescent inorganic pigments

GRANULATES containing fluorescent
organic pigments

THREADS with fluorescent organic pigments

INTERMEDIATE OR END PRODUCTS

PAPER e.g. with fluorescent organic pigments

FILM e.g. with fluorescent inks

CARPET e.g. from fluorescent wool

CLOTH e.g. from fluorescent yarns

Paints made from UV-luminous inorganic pigments:

ALCOHOL-BASED UV LIQUIDS
They can be applied to textiles and other absorbent materials by soaking.
✚ Good adhesion.
▬ Limited lightfastness.

To ensure the long service life of the product and to improve colour intensity, the products should not be applied too thinly. The colours light blue and light yellow are suitable for indoor use only as they luminesce under artificial ultraviolet light only. Resistance to abrasion can be increased by the application of an additional protective coating, for example, a transparent lacquer.

Granulates from daylight-luminous organic pigments:

GRANULATES (COMPOUNDS) BASED ON POLYACRYL
They can be heated and cast or injection moulded into different shapes.
✚ Accurate batching, can be processed with other polyacryl-based granulates.
▬ Limited lightfastness

Threads from daylight-luminous organic pigments:

POLYACRYL-BASED WOOL (WOOL YARN)
They can be processed manually and by machine into various textile fabrics.
✚ Can be processed like ordinary wool and with other types of wool.
▬ Limited lightfastness.

POLYESTER-BASED YARNS (SEWING YARNS, SPUN YARNS)
They can be processed manually and by machine to form various textile fabrics and seams.
✚ Can be processed like ordinary yarn and with other types of yarn.
▬ Limited lightfastness

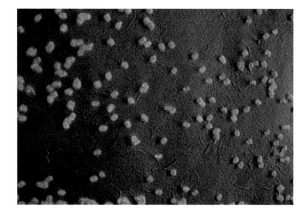

fluorescence › projects

Fluorescent products of interest in architectural applications, in particular for interiors, include daylight-luminous dispersion-based paints, specially for wall paints on plaster substrates, and daylight-luminous films that can be applied to smooth substrates such as door panels, tiles, floor coverings, metal cladding etc.

As fluorescent coatings and claddings would gradually become bleached over the longer term and this leads to an irreversible loss of function, steps should be taken to reduce exposure to damaging energy radiation peaks, both in summer and winter. This can be achieved by applying the coatings in sheltered areas only or by constructional measures, for example, by using selective elements (filters) to place the coatings behind temporary or permanent features that reflect or filter sunlight.

In recent years some aesthetically impressive works exploring the theme of fluorescence have been produced by designers and artists.

Paper with blue fluorescent granulate, paper with green fluorescent yarns: *UV-Lichtpapier*, Anke Neumann. | Fluorescent film: *Creeping Buttercup*, Ruth Handschin.

Luminous Drawing

Monosmart material | Monosmart application
Light-emitting smart material:
PAPER WITH FLUORESCENT INK
Fluorescent wall surfaces

Ruth Handschin, Germany
Light installation | Künstlerhaus Bethanien, Berlin,
Germany (1990)

Her installation *Leuchtzeichnung* (Luminous drawing), shown
in 1990 in the Künstlerhaus Bethanien art centre in Berlin,
was the first major public work of the Swiss artist Ruth
Handschin. Consisting of a tangle of crossing double lines
with embedded random shapes, some serrated, some rounded, the work is reminiscent of the outlines of a road network
populated by insect-like organisms.

Ruth Handschin describes her work as "nocturnal." She wrote
about it in 1990:

"Pale by day, scarcely visible, (the drawing) starts to luminesce at dusk. First light yellow on light violet-grey, then later
in full darkness, shocking yellow on violet-blue. The human
eye, overloaded by this extreme contrast of bright and dark,
begins to leap from line to line. The whole network raises itself off the floor and walls."

The installation consists of fluorescent strips of paper, which
are precisely cut on site then stuck on to two walls, two col-
umns and the floor of the exhibition room and excited by UV
light. The effect is distorted to an extent which depends on
the position of the observer in the room and the angle of
view of the *Leuchtzeichnung*. Only when viewed from one
particular position can the *Leuchtzeichnung* be seen as a
true two-dimensional, undistorted luminous surface.

Leuchtzeichnung from different angles.

TWO ROOMS

Monosmart material | Monosmart application
Light-emitting smart material:
PAINT WITH FLUORESCENT PIGMENTS
Fluorescent window surfaces

Christina Kubisch, Germany
Light installation | Theatre Altes Schloss Ettersburg, Weimar,
Germany (2004)

Near Weimar, in the man-made natural surroundings of one of the English-style parks designed by Prince Pückler-Muskau, stand the old and new chateaux of Schloss Ettersburg, which were used in summer 2004 as part of a newly established festival by artists Christina Kubisch and Bernhard Leitner for their exhibition "Zeitversetzt" ("Shifted in Time"). Given that the chateaux were located in the immediate vicinity of the Buchenwald concentration camp and requisitioned by the SS in February 1945, the intention was to revive the cultural tradition by giving attention to this particular history.

For one of her three installations Christina Kubisch chose a large glass window, which was located behind the stage of a room formerly used as a theatre in the west wing of the old chateau. Inspired by the rooms, the events of earlier times and the idea of bringing the stage back to life for a short time, the artist created an installation of light and sound. She applied a special fluorescent coating to the large glass window, in three-parts and divided by bars, which had at its rear face a brightly lit corridor; the corridor and had originally provided a form of background lighting. The aim of the design was to create "fragile layers of time."

The coating, which, when looked at more closely, is reminiscent of frosted glass and consists of several wafer-thin glazes of greenish white fluorescent pigment with an unspecified binder, was applied over several days to cover the individual glass panes. Four UV lamps, which were concealed so that they could not be localised by the observer, were used to activate the pigment in the coating. A black cloth was suspended over the corridor-facing rear face of the wall to darken the stage and the visitors' room.

Together with the sounds of a glass harmonica, sometimes occurring individually, sometimes overlapping at irregular intervals, *Zwei Räume* (Two Rooms) gives the impression of an "imaginary theatre piece," in which the luminous surface is the stage and the characters enter in the form of sounds.

Zwei Räume (Two Rooms): detail of the fluorescent coating. | Window front of the theatre from outside, untreated. | Window front of the theatre from inside, fluorescent coating.

Lost Embryo

Monosmart material | Monosmart application
Light-emitting smart material:
YARN WITH FLUORESCENT PIGMENTS
Fluorescent wall surfaces

EunSook Lee, Germany
Light installation | Embassy of the Republic of Korea,
Berlin and elsewhere, Germany (2003)

During the preparations for her first exhibition in 1986, Korean artist EunSook Lee suffered severe burns, which threatened to rob her of all movement in her right hand. Traumatised by this event she tried to incorporate her inner conflicts, anxieties and pains into her subsequent projects. With her installation *Lost Embryo* EunSook Lee was able to visually express the depths of her feelings and her love of nature in a fantastic way.

Lost Embryo, first presented to the public in 1999 in Vancouver, Canada, attempts to represent artistically the inside of an over-sized womb. Between 600 and 700 embryos are symbolised by 20 cm long, convoluted tubular shapes and attached in a grid pattern to the full room height, monochrome walls at intervals of about 25 cm. Each individual tubular shape is made up of numerous fluorescent threads which are thermally laminated between two transparent polyester strips and patched together to form convoluted three-dimensional tubes. This creates areas where the fluorescent threads are overlaid by the polyester material, and other areas where the threads are not laminated and therefore fully exposed. The use of different colours for the threads and polyester strips, excited by the long ultraviolet lighting tubes attached to the ceiling, creates a fascinating interplay of form and colour.

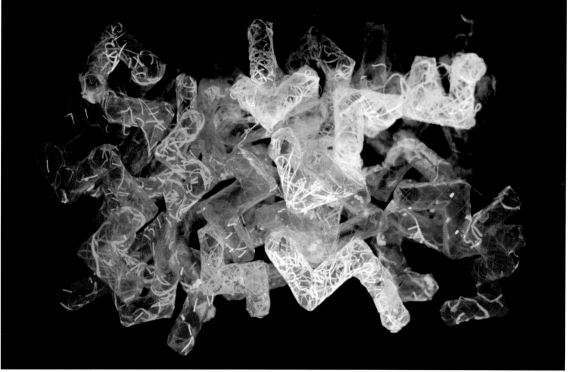

Lost Embryo: general view. | Detail of fluorescent threads in the tubular structures.

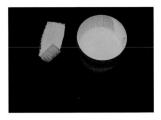

Alkaline earth aluminate crystals. | Phosphorescent paint by day and at night. | Granulate (compound) and a polyacryl-based plastic profile produced from it.

phosphorescence › materials

In contrast to fluorescence the optical phenomenon of phosphorescence in materials or components involves some afterglow luminescence. This occurs when a molecule absorbs light and emits light again during the transition from an excited triplet state to the ground state over a period of greater than 10^{-8} seconds ([11]). Materials or components that have this ability to persistently emit light are described as phosphors.

Depending on the length of the afterglow luminescence process, the phosphorescent materials or components can be differentiated into:

PHOSPHORESCENT MATERIALS OR COMPONENTS
These materials luminesce for a comparatively short time and have only a slight excitement sensitivity.

Some phosphorescent materials or components are:

INORGANIC MATERIALS OR COMPONENTS
Zinc sulphide crystals, magnesium sulphide crystals.

PERSISTENTLY PHOSPHORESCENT MATERIALS OR COMPONENTS (AFTERGLOWS)
These materials luminesce for a comparatively long time and have high excitement sensitivity.

Some persistently phosphorescent materials or components are:

INORGANIC MATERIALS OR COMPONENTS
Rare earths (e.g. alkaline earth aluminate crystals)

Phosphorescent materials also include:

MINERALS
Lapis Solaris ("Bolognian Phosphorus")

As these materials or components also absorb the ultraviolet radiation contained in daylight and emit it as light, luminescence may persist, with sufficient excitement, even on days when no or only inadequate further excitement is taking place. This is the case in particular for alkaline earth aluminate crystals.

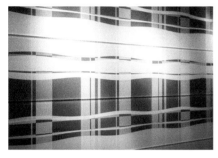

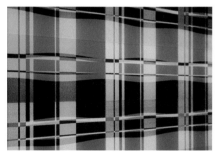

Phosphorescent glass blocks (Veluna). |
Phosphorescent glass tiles (Onda) by
day and at night.

The following are currently of interest to architecture:

ZINC SULPHIDE CRYSTALS, MAGNESIUM SULPHIDE CRYSTALS
These materials are excited by natural and artificial light, and by radiation from radioactive substances. After excitation ceases the luminance falls to 10% or less of its original value within 20 minutes.
＋ Market presence, can be made in large quantities, many years of practical use, high brilliance and intensity of colour, very short excitement time (a few minutes), long afterglow (several hours), no radioactive substances, no lead or chromium pigments, versatile range of applications; depending on type, resistance to particular chemicals and high temperatures, also available in small quantities, inexpensive compared to alkaline earth aluminate crystals.
－ Limited lightfastness.

ALKALINE EARTH ALUMINATE CRYSTALS
These materials are excited by natural and artificial light, and by radiation from radioactive substances.
＋ Market presence, very high brilliance and intensity of colour, short excitement time, very long afterglow (several hours), versatile range of applications, resistance to particular chemicals and very high temperatures, available in small quantities.
－ Expensive compared to zinc sulphide crystals or magnesium sulphide crystals.

phosphorescence › products

The first phosphorescent products were timepieces and instruments that were mainly used by the military. Dial faces and hands were given a luminous coating that normally contained radioactive substances. Until 1950 this was mainly radium-226, while from 1950 cheaper strontium-90 and yttrium-90 were used, which resulted in wrist complaints due to beta radiation. Today, for the manufacturing of phosphorescent products the above-mentioned zinc sulphide, magnesium sulphide and alkaline earth aluminate crystals are used. They have been developed for a wide range of applications and are mature products on the market.

In architecture there is particular interest in the following products involving phosphorescent inorganic pigments, some of which can be applied directly to walls, for example, or which can be processed into further products:

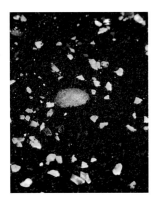

Currently available or developed
products useful in architecture include:

RAW OR END PRODUCTS

INORGANIC PIGMENTS from e.g.
zinc sulphide crystals

PAINTS containing phosphorescent
inorganic pigments

GRANULATES containing phosphorescent
inorganic pigments

THREADS containing phosphorescent
inorganic pigments

INTERMEDIATE OR END PRODUCTS

PAPER with e.g. phosphorescent
inorganic pigments

FILMS with e.g. phosphorescent
inorganic inks

CONCRETE with e.g. phosphorescent
inorganic pigments

GLASS with e.g. phosphorescent
inorganic pigments

PLASTICS with e.g. phosphorescent
inorganic pigments (e.g. polycarbonate panels)

FABRICS with e.g. phosphorescent threads

FABRICS incorporating metal with e.g.
phosphorescent threads

Paints containing phosphorescent inorganic pigments:

PHOSPHORESCENT DISPERSION-BASED PAINTS
They can be applied by brush, roller or spray to surfaces such as wood, plastic, textiles, paper, cardboard, concrete and masonry.
+ High flexibility, good adhesion.
– Limited lightfastness.

PHOSPHORESCENT PAINTS BASED ON TWO-COMPONENT ACRYLATE-BASED PAINT
They can be applied by brush, roller or spray to surfaces such as metal, wood and glass.
+ Good resistance to mechanical loads, good adhesion, good dirt resistance, simple to clean, resistance to wear with an additional protective lacquer.
– Limited lightfastness.

General recommendations for use:
The luminous effect depends not only on the pigment used but also considerably on the concentration, application surface, coating thickness and the colour of the substrate. The abrasion resistance of the paint can be enhanced by the application of a transparent protective lacquer.

FILMS
Laminate comprising a white primer, the phosphorescent layer and a UV-stabilised transparent finishing coat.
+ Can be used in low to medium temperature ranges (–40°C to +80°C), available in various luminous intensities and film thicknesses.
– Limited lightfastness (outside), limited choice of colour (predominantly green).

Granulates containing persistently phosphorescent inorganic pigments:

GRANULATES (COMPOUNDS, ENCAPSULATED MASTER BATCHES) BASED ON POLYETHYL VINYL ACETATE
They can be incorporated into various thermoplastics such as PE, PP, PVC, PES, ABS, PA, PC, PMMA, duroplastics such as PES, PUR and amino plastics, and heated for casting or injection moulding into various shapes.
+ High excitement sensitivity, very long persistence, can be used in low to medium temperature ranges (–40°C to +80°C), largely lightfast (outside), accurate batching, can be processed with other thermoplastic-based granulates.
– Limited choice of colour (predominantly green).

Complex three-dimensional shapes, which could be of particular interest in wall claddings, can be manufactured using compounds or master batches capable of being heated.

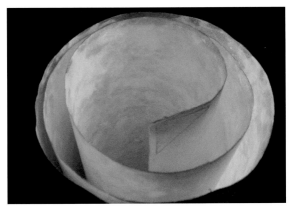

Threads with phosphorescent inorganic pigments:

POLYACRYL-BASED WOOL (WOOL YARN)
They can be processed manually and by machine into various textile fabrics.
+ Can be processed like ordinary wool and with other types of wool.
− Limited lightfastness.

POLYESTER-BASED YARNS (SEWING YARNS, SPUN YARNS)
They can be processed manually and by machine to form various textile fabrics and seams.
+ Can be processed like ordinary yarn and with other types of yarn.
− Limited lightfastness.

With suitable yarns, phosphorescent textile fabrics such as curtains, roller blinds, vertical blinds, wall coverings or room dividers can be manufactured. Wool yarns can be used e.g. in carpets, seating or textile wall coverings.

phosphorescence › projects

Phosphorescent paints are currently mainly used in architecture for safety-related applications, like marking escape routes with directional arrows or as a visibility aid on the front edges of stairs. By the use of appropriate materials and products in their projects, for example in spatial installations, artists, and increasingly designers and architects, are confronting the wider public with more than the conventional applications.

Footway covering with phosphorescent glass fragments and other luminescent components: *Maya Mountain Street*, Kobe, Kirakira-Komichi. | Paper with green phosphorescent pigments: *Phos-Licht-Papier*, Anke Neumann. | *opposite:* Phosphorescent pavement.

Luminous Room

Polysmart materials | Monosmart application
Light-emitting smart materials:
PAINT WITH FLUORESCENT AND PHOSPHORESCENT PIGMENTS
Fluorescent and phosphorescent wall, ceiling and floor surfaces

Ruth Handschin, Germany
Light installation | Hotel Teufelhof, Basel, Switzerland (1994)

At the Teufelhof Hotel in Basel, Monica and Dominique Thommy-Kneschaurek seek to provide a gastronomic as well as a cultural experience to their guests. In addition to the gastronomy area there is a theatre, a "gallery hotel," and an „art hotel". In the latter each one of the eight rooms is made into a walk-in work of art. The rooms are completely redesigned roughly every three years. For the redesign in July and August 1994 the artist Ruth Handschin provided one of the rooms with various light drawings, turning it into a *Leuchtzimmer* (Luminous Room).

The drawings were created using a mixture of fluorescent and phosphorescent pigments, which were applied as paint with an acrylic binder in thin lines on the ceiling, wall and floor. The large format motifs depict the outlines of leaves and extend over several surfaces. By the addition of various types of luminescent pigments the motifs emit light both day and night. They use the ultraviolet radiation contained in natural light over the day, and at night give up, after a delay, the natural and/or artificial light taken in during the day.

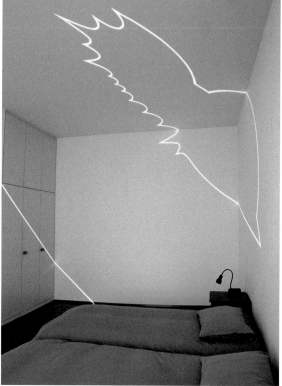

Leuchtzimmer: luminous drawings by day. | Luminous drawings at night.

Filigree wallpaper

> Monosmart material | Monosmart application
> Light-emitting smart material:
> **PAINT (SUGAR SOLUTION) WITH PHOSPHORESCENT PIGMENTS**
> Phosphorescent wall surface

Juliet Quintero, Great Britain
Luminous wallpaper | Great Britain (2004)

"Everything around her was different. The house, the countryside, the people. She had entered a fairytale world that would become more and more real for her".

Alice in Wonderland was the unusual design theme of Juliet Quintero, who in 2004 studied with Jonathan Hill at the Bartlett School of Architecture, UCL, London. Equally unusual was the material that was to contribute to the transformation of her work, which was called "Alice's House": sugar. Everything possible in "Alice's House" was to be made completely or in part from sugar: the walls, the wallpaper, the panes of glass, the curtains, the mirror. It was to be left to change over time in the London mist, smog, rain and/or light and in this way undergo a transformation. Instead of traditional building materials, the artificial stone was made out of caramelised sugar and the glass from invert sugar. Curtains were given more materiality by stiffening and thus became more immediate. This was achieved by filling the sewn curtain materials with sugar, which was then crystallised out by moistening and drying.

Filigree Wallpaper is based on a wallpaper design by William Morris. The paint was a sugar solution made of egg white mixed with royal icing sugar, hot water and phosphorescent pigments, which was applied to a sheet of glass following the wallpaper pattern. Contrary to expectations, the addition of pigments and the egg white component did not have any moisture-stabilising effect. The sugar component did not lose its inherent hygroscopic property, which means the paint has remained extremely sensitive so that *Filigree Wallpaper* is mainly suitable for interiors and the paint for indoor application.

The properties of the added phosphorescent pigments on the other hand were successfully preserved: *Filigree Wallpaper* luminesced after 15 minutes of excitement by natural light.

Filigree Wallpaper by day and at night.

SHUSH night lights

Monosmart material | Monosmart application
Light-emitting smart material:
MIXED FABRIC WITH PHOSPHORESCENT THREADS
Phosphorescent lights, room dividers and curtains

Hannaliisa Hailahti, Finland
Luminous fabric | Finland (2005)

Finnish designer Hannaliisa Hailahti developed a fine luminous fabric made from phosphorescent and metallic silver reflective threads. The designer sought a vision for energy-autonomous lighting elements with the aim of creating a more appealing nocturnal atmosphere and allowing safe movement around the house at night without the use of further light sources; at the same time she wanted to avoid complete darkness.

In the dark, the light emitted from the phosphorescent threads is reflected by the adjacent metallic threads to increase the luminous effect. The bending stiffness of the metal allows the fabric to be hand-formed into different shapes. Depending on the cut and the dimensions, this kind of fabric can be used as lights, room dividers or curtains.

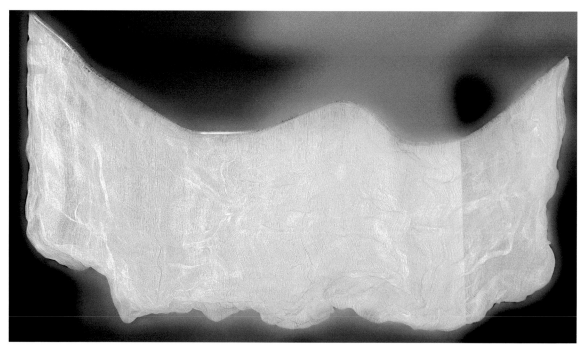

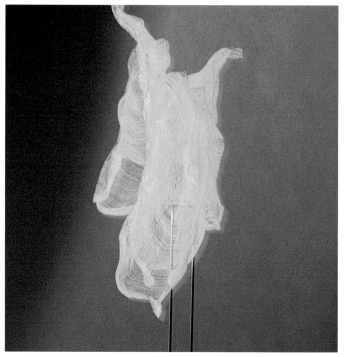

Shush as an unfolded room divider at night and closed by day. |
Shush as a luminous source.

ELECTROLUMINESCENT SMART MATERIALS >
MATERIALS, PRODUCTS, PROJECTS

An optical phenomenon in which a molecule emits light
due to the effect of the electrons in an electrical field.

Based on the current stage of development electroluminescence can be differentiated as follows:

INJECTION ELECTROLUMINESCENCE

POWDER ELECTROLUMINESCENCE

THIN FILM ELECTROLUMINESCENCE

THICK FILM ELECTROLUMINESCENCE

POLYMER-/SMALL MOLECULE
ELECTROLUMINESCENCE

Materials and products from the field of injection-, thick
film- and polymer-/small molecule electroluminescence
are considered in detail below. The latter are currently
in the market introduction phase.

injection electroluminescence |
light-emitting diodes (LED) › materials

Injection electroluminescence is the fundamental principle behind semiconductor light sources
such as light-emitting diodes (LED), in which the charge carriers are introduced from outside
by a so-called injection current and light is emitted by the recombination of electrons and
holes.

Doped gallium arsenide acts as the lumminescent material in LEDs. It is embedded between
two electrodes which are encapsulated by light-transparent plastic to separate them from their
surroundings. For a long time only red, yellow and green LEDs were available, but with the development of blue LEDs, which has only recently extended the range of possible light colours,
now even white LEDs can be produced by combinations of different light colours.

French scientist Georges Destriau discovered electroluminescence (EL) as early as 1936. It remained in the laboratory however until the late 1960s. The aim had been to develop an alternative to incandescent bulbs as a light source; this was not an initial success.

Electroluminescent materials or components in the field of injection electroluminescence
include:

INORGANIC COMPOUNDS
Doped gallium arsenide, other gallium compounds.

The following is currently of interest to architecture:

DOPED GALLIUM ARSENIDE
This semiconductor is doped with different metals. The method used for production, crystal growth, is expensive.
+ Market presence, many years of practical use, high brilliance and intensity of colour, in its encapsulated version free of toxic substances, versatile range of applications; depending on type, resistance to particular chemicals and high temperatures, also available in small quantities.
− Only manufactured by a few specialist factories, limited number of available light colours.

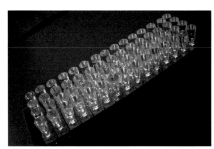

injection electroluminescence |
light-emitting diodes (LED) › products

The first use of light-emitting diodes (LED) was in electronic devices, where for many years they were utilized for function control and operational data displays. Today the aim is to restrict the number of LEDs in applications where previously a high number of LEDs had been used, such as in cars, which often had up to 200 LEDs. This is done by using a single or a few centralised light sources with connected flexible fibre-optic cables to illuminate the various positions.

In a manner similar to fibre-optic cables, glass or transparent plastic panels, e.g. PMMA, are used for illumination; with these techniques LEDs attached to the end faces direct their light into the main faces of the panels. This arrangement avoids any impression of point light sources, which would be the case with LEDs incorporated into the main panel faces. Taking the opposite approach, by arranging the LEDs densely in the main face in relation to the viewing distance and having individual control of each LED, combinations of various colours of LED can produce coloured or even white moving film sequences comparable to television pictures. In recent times this application has become increasingly popular as a replacement for conventional large projected images, e.g. in the entertainment field.

Depending on their different output classes LED can be categorised as:

STANDARD LED
These LEDs can be soldered or inserted into circuit boards or clamped or screwed to electrically conductive substrates, cables etc.
+ Comparatively long replacement life, comparatively low power consumption, versatile range of applications, generally resistant to particular chemicals and high temperatures, also available in small quantities, comparatively inexpensive.
− No ability to illuminate areas, limited number of available light colours.

If necessary, the luminous effect can be increased by the use of lenses etc. Where there is restricted room for installation, small diameter light-transmitting glass or plastic can be placed in front of the LEDs. Special LEDs are available for use outdoors.

2 W high output LEDs | RGB multi-LED. | High output LEDs with optical lenses. | Complex arrangement of light sources formed with several LEDs for a car. | Lamp with high output LED. | Colour-on-demand LED. | *opposite:* LEDs in plastic housing (Solarbrick). | LEDs in glass. | Facade with LEDs in plastic housings in combination with solar cells: South Korea. | LEDs in metal mesh (Mediamesh) | Highrise facade with LEDs in and before stainless steel mesh (Mediamesh and Illumesh): project by Benjamin Romana.

HIGH OUTPUT LED
As they have been developed for a wide range of applications, they are available with a number of different connection types. They can be used in architecture wherever high light output is required and the necessary electrical energy is available.
+ Can provide up to 100 times the light output of standard LEDs.
− Cannot be used everywhere, comparatively expensive.

Several LEDs are combined into one unit for particular applications. They can be supplied in modules, clusters etc. and fitted with optical lenses for combining the emitted light, for example.

injection electroluminescence | light-emitting diodes (LED) › projects

Standard light-emitting diodes (LED) are finding increasing use in architecture. Ultraflat LEDs integrated into glass panes that can be supplied with electricity through almost invisible cable-ways are used for illuminating transparent balustrades, banisters, room dividers etc.

Currently available or developed products useful in architecture include:

RAW OR END PRODUCTS

STANDARD LEDs

HIGH OUTPUT LEDs

RGB multi-LEDs

COLOUR-ON-DEMAND LEDs

INTERMEDIATE OR END PRODUCTS

GLASS with LEDs

GLASS with LEDs in combination with solar cells

METAL FABRIC with LEDs

PLASTIC FABRIC with LEDs

Hotel Habitat H&R

Polysmart materials | Monosmart application
Light-emitting smart materials:
METAL FABRIC WITH LED, SOLAR CELLS
Colour and light changes dependent on light and software

CLOUD 9, Spain
Light-kinetic curtain-wall facade | Hotel Habitat H&R, Barcelona,
Spain (2007)

"Your room in a tree" is the concept for a new hotel to be completed in the
Hospitalet district of Barcelona by 2007. The future guests and staff will
enjoy the benefits of an artificial forest of leaves that forms the external skin
of the new *Hotel Habitat H&R*. The building, designed by Spanish architect
Ruiz-Geli and his CLOUD 9 practice with other partners, consists of a comparatively simple highrise with a conventional glass facade, which is covered
with a stainless steel mesh on which a multitude of artificial leaves with
electronics are attached.

Placed at a distance of 57 cm apart, each of these 5000 25 cm diameter
leaves is fitted with a solar cell. The electrical current created during the day
is stored temporarily in an accumulator and directed to one-, two- or three-
RGB LEDs at night by a processor (CPU). The processor analyses the state
of charge of the accumulator and the energy consumption of the LEDs, and
controls the duration of illumination appropriately for one, two or three
LEDs. By using LED combinations, a total of seven colours can be created:
in addition to the standard colours red, green and blue achieved by switching
on the appropriate single LED in each case, combinations of two LEDs produce the colours magenta, yellow and cyan, while switching on all three LEDs
gives a white light.

Depending on the season and the energetic conditions, at night the building
skin will change automatically by putting on illuminated clothes of different
colours.

Hotel Habitat H&R: illustration of general view.

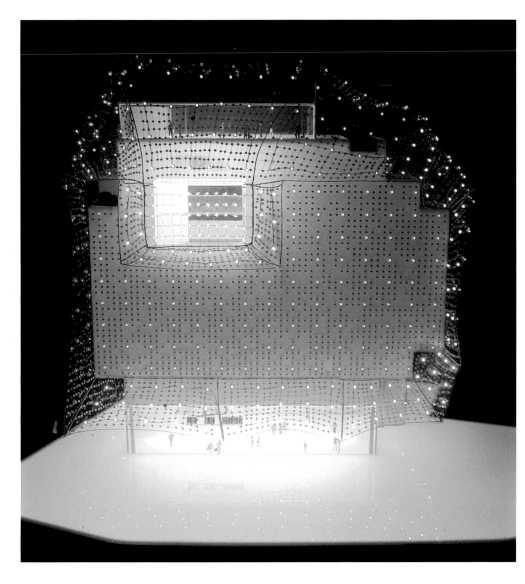

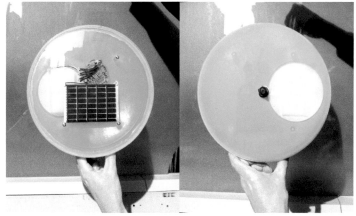

Hotel Habitat H&R: illuminated model. | Partial view of model. | Prototype of an artificial leaf with solar cell, RGB LEDs, processor and accumulator. | Basic colours of artificial leaves (red, green, blue and white).

thick film electroluminescence | electro-luminescent materials (EL) › materials

Thick film electroluminescence is a possible principle of operation for in most cases flat light sources made from electroluminescent material (EL). It is based on the interaction of several functional layers. The thickness of the light-emitting layer, also called the emitter layer, is much thicker than that used in thin film technology. When an electrical field is applied, the deposited luminous pigment (phosphorus) is excited and emits a cold light. EL films and EL cables are two of the products developed from this technology.

ELs or components in the field of thick film electroluminescence include:

INORGANIC COMPOUNDS
Doped zinc sulphide.

The following are currently of interest to architecture:

DOPED ZINC SULPHIDE
This is a semiconductor doped with different metals to create different colours of light, which can be applied to plastic and glass.
+ Market presence, years of practical use, also available in small quantities, comparatively inexpensive.
– A relatively high alternating current is required, limited number of available light colours.

thick film electroluminescence | electro-luminescent materials (EL) › products

Unlike those based on thin film technology, thick film technology products have established themselves on the market, although their design principle is virtually identical. Both mix the luminescent pigments with a transparent, organic or ceramic binder. To apply an electrical field to the top (layer) a very thin transparent, electrically conductive metal layer is used as a front electrode and an electrically conductive metal layer as the back electrode. The construction is the same as a capacitor, which is why they are also called luminescence diodes.

EL cable. | EL film. | EL ink printed on speedometer.

Originally in competition with the incandescent light bulbs, which as well as emitting visible light convert the majority of the absorbed energy into heat and like LEDs provide a point source of light, they were developed first as luminescent film, also called EL film, which emits cold area light from its surface. Later came electroluminescent material (EL) strips and EL cables, which were developed using the same principle. An important advantage over incandescent light bulbs is that by using suitably flexible layer components even curved substrates can be clad with appropriate products.

EL products are used for backlighting LCD displays, as liquid crystals cannot emit light themselves. Further areas of application include luminous advertising boards, safety-related products etc.

The following are of current and future interest to architecture:

EL FILM
One-sided and double-sided luminous films are available. They can be used on flat and on curved substrates and can be attached mechanically or by adhesives. One variant is EL strip.
⊞ Comparatively long replacement life, comparatively low power consumption, versatile fields of application, generally resistant to moisture and high temperatures (< −20°C to > +50°C), some resistance to UV light, also available in small quantities, comparatively inexpensive, can be customised in various ways, infinitely dimmable, can be operated using low voltages, light, unbreakable, smooth flicker-free luminous surfaces, impact resistance, very short reaction times.
⊟ Alternating current supply required, additional electronics required, cannot be bent to shape.

Film can be cut with scissors to create complex luminous shapes without affecting functionality. The electricity supply electronics must be suitably adjusted to volume of power consumption and size of the luminous surface area.

EL CABLE
They can be attached to surfaces by staples, adhesives or by sewing.
⊞ Comparatively long replacement life, can be used in low to medium temperatures (< −20°C to > +50°C), 360° light emission, comparatively high mechanical loading capacity, available up to 250 m long.
⊟ Alternating current supply required, additional electronics required, cannot be bent to shape.

The general recommendations for use are those for EL film.

Currently available or developed products useful in architecture include:

RAW OR END PRODUCTS

EL FILM, EL STRIP

EL CABLE

EL INKS, PRINTING INKS

INTERMEDIATE OR END PRODUCTS

PAPER with EL CABLES

FABRIC with EL PRINT

PANELS with EL PRINT

METAL FABRIC with EL CABLES

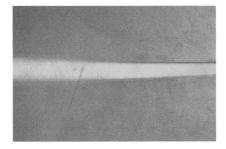

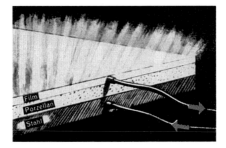

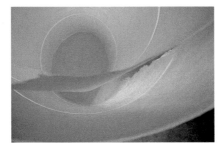

Model room with EL panels from 1957. |
Illustration of the "Electron lights" (1957) |
Paper with EL strips: *Ellum-Lichtpapier*,
Anke Neumann.

EL INKS
Can be applied to various surfaces using printing techniques, usually the silk-screen printing process.
◼ Can be used in low to medium temperatures (< –20°C to > +50°C) and for comparatively complex luminous surfaces.
◼ Specialist manufacture necessary.

thick film electroluminescence | electro-luminescent materials (EL) › projects

The first architectural use of electroluminescent material (EL) elements was in 1957. 112 square luminous surfaces were built into a model room. Glass and other materials were used in the panels. Evidence that such panels were already commercially available is to be found in an article in the German magazine *Hobby – Das Magazin der Technik* ([12]) entitled: "...und es leuchten die Wände" (and the walls provide the light). The walls were made from sheet metal and porcelain; phosphorus crystals were used as the luminous medium.

EL films are currently used in architecture in interiors and exteriors. Although they are now mass-produced and the available dimensions have continuously increased, currently the only way to create relatively large luminous surfaces is by grouping several smaller EL films together. Uses for EL films and EL strips include large format displays in public areas, luminous floor coverings, e.g. in television studios and in works of art.

EL cable can be used to create shapes and edges on buildings or for creating linear features on luminous surfaces or luminous pictures on facades.

EL inks offer the architect a lot of possibilities. They can, for example, be applied using the silk-screen printing process as a coloured pattern to facade elements. The images can be created on a personal computer or scanned.

Flowers

Monosmart material | Monosmart application
Light-emitting smart material:
FABRIC WITH EL PRINT
Illuminations depending on light and software

Loop.pH Ltd. – Rachel Wingfield, Mathias Gmachl,
Great Britain
Light-kinetic room dividers | Great Britain (2004)

The work *Blumen* (Flowers) by designers Rachel Wingfield
and Mathias Gmachl at their company Loop.pH Ltd. in London shows how traditional decorative floral patterns can be
used in conjunction with EL technology for the development
of innovative room dividers.

The room dividers, which were first developed as functional
technology demonstrators, consist of several similar shaped,
wide, textile louvres suspended from the ceiling. They are
arranged side by side to open in a space-saving manner in
their own guide rails.

The pattern consists of a four-part leaf motif that, when reflected eight times, forms a square basic shape and is arranged in a larger square pattern, which in its turn, depending on the desired louvre dimensions, can be extended by
simply adding more patterns to the sides or above and below.
The pattern was made to luminesce by an electroluminescent ink, which was applied to the textile using a special
inkjet printer. Thin electrical wire, different in colour and
made to surround the individual patterned areas ornamen-
tally, allows each area to be individually supplied with current and hence controlled.

With specially developed software the room dividers can be
designed to react to various stimuli depending on the characteristics of the sensors used. It would be possible for example to have room dividers in which a varying number of
areas would luminesce, depending on the current state of
light conditions. With the right control system the patterned
areas could illuminate to create their own patterns.

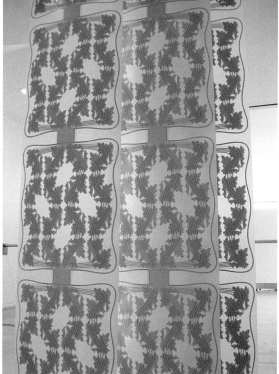

Blumen room divider with a section of pattern (technology
demonstrator). | Detailed photograph of *Blumen* room divider. |
Partial, pattern-forming illumination of individual patterned
areas.

weather patterns

Monosmart material | Monosmart application
Light-emitting smart material:
PANELS WITH EL PRINT
Illuminations depending on light and software

Loop.pH Ltd. – Rachel Wingfield, Mathias Gmachl, Great Britain
Light installation | York Art Gallery, London, Great Britain (2005-2010)

This light installation, on display since October 2005 and intended to last for five years at the York Art Gallery in London, during the night converts the local weather events into visual effects on the building, where they can be witnessed by passers-by. It demonstrates the combination of traditional shapes with contemporary display technology based on electroluminescence. Five horizontally aligned display panels are placed in the recesses of the narrow false windows in the upper storey of the art gallery facade, above the entrance to the classical Italian Renaissance-style building.

Each of the displays consists of a panel printed with electroluminescent inks and encapsulated between a sheet of hardened glass and a mirror. To visualise the different weather conditions an ornamental-looking, square weather map was designed in which, according to the sensory data provided, concentric spiral-shaped areas can be switched on and off by a computer programmed with specially developed software.

Weather data is collected by a compact weather station; in this case a Davis-Vantage Pro2 with sensors for atmospheric pressure, temperature, humidity, rainfall as well as wind speed and direction. It is positioned on the portico roof over the entrance.

The aim of this installation is to draw the nocturnal passer-by's attention, by means of the aesthetic and kinematic of the light patterns, to the global warming caused by Man.

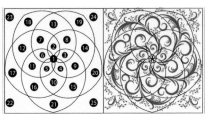

Weather Patterns: complete pattern. | Different sections of pattern that can be activated. | Possible patterns depend on the weather conditions. | *Weather Patterns* by day and at night.

polymer/small molecule electro-luminescence ı organic light-emitting diodes (OLED) › materials

Organic light-emitting diodes (OLED) are normally manufactured as flat LEDs based on organic, semiconductor polymers, or small molecules, which like the latter emit cold light by the absorption of electrons.

Depending on the components used, organic LEDs manufactured with polymers are given the abbreviation PLEDs or POLEDs, and those OLEDs manufactured with small molecules the abbreviations SOLEDs or SMOLEDs. OLEDs with particular flexibility or those in which phosphorescent components are used are sometimes also called FOLEDs or PHOLEDs respectively.

OLEDs generally consist of several functional layers placed one upon the other. The bottom layer, e.g. a glass plate, acts as a substrate to carry the layers above it. On this goes the anode, e.g. indium tin oxide (ITO). On top of this follows the hole transport layer (HTL). Another layer may be applied between the ITO and the HTL layers. In some cases this layer may be used to produce a smooth surface. On top of the HTL layer there is another layer, known as the emitter layer (EL), which is formed with a small amount of pigment (approx. 5% to 10%) or may consist of 100% pigment. On top of this comes the electron transport layer (ETL), on which a cathode of e.g. calcium or aluminium is deposited. Finally a covering layer is applied, e.g. a glass plate.

Application of an electrical field causes the pigment in the emitter layer, where positive and negative charges meet (known as the recombination layer), to be excited and emit white or coloured cold light, depending on the pigment used.

The first designs for OLEDs were produced in the USA, where an international photographic company submitted the first patent application in the 1980s. The patent application was for organic luminous diodes based on small molecules deposited in a vacuum (SMOLED). In 1990, electroluminescence was discovered in polymers and OLEDs were then also made using Cambridge Display Technology processes, in which long-chain polymers are applied by rotation coating or pressure coating on to an electrode (POLED). Since then there have been numerous developments of OLEDs mainly in the USA, Japan and Germany. Today sees the two technologies in competition with each other.

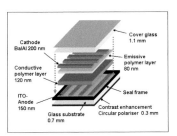

Schematic representation of the construction of a SMOLED and a POLED.

Materials and components generally used for SMOLEDs include among others:

SMALL MOLECULES
E.g. aluminium-tris(8-hydroxyquinoline) (Alq_3), aluminium-tris(8-hydroxyquinoline) (Alq_3) + polymer.

Materials and components generally used for POLEDs include among others:

ORGANIC, SEMICONDUCTING POLYMERS
E.g. polyphenylenvinylene (PPV), polythiophene and polyfluorene (green, red and blue fluorescent pigments).

INORGANIC-ORGANIC, SEMICONDUCTING POLYMERS
Metal-organic complexes (phosphorescent pigments).

The following are of interest to architecture:

ALUMINIUM-TRIS(8-HYDROXYQUINOLINE) (ALQ_3)
Organic semiconductors, suitable for the manufacture of colour displays and light sources, can be applied to various substrates such as glass and plastic.
＋ Market presence, many years of practical use, relatively good optical properties, low electrical voltage required (e.g. 3V to 5V).
－ Relatively expensive manufacturing process under vacuum conditions and therefore comparatively expensive to use.

POLYPHENYLENVINYLENE (PPV), POLYTHIOPHENE, POLYFLUORENE
Organic semiconductor polymers luminescent in RGB colours, suitable for the manufacture of colour displays and light sources, can be applied to various substrates such as glass and plastic.
＋ Market presence, many years of practical use, relatively good photoconductivity and electroluminescence, low electrical voltage required (e.g. 3V to 5V).
－ Limited number of available luminous colours.

Green and red crystals as p- and n-dopants for the manufacture of SMOLEDs.

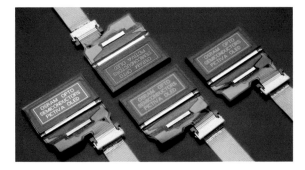

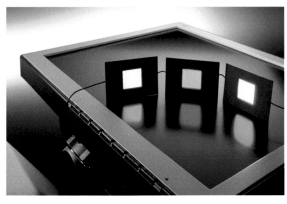

polymer/small molecule electroluminescence ı organic light-emitting diodes (ᴏʟᴇᴅ) › products

As the principle of this type of electroluminescence is comparatively new and still has a certain number of weak points, like the in many cases inadequate long-term stability for some colours and its moisture susceptibility, there are only a few products available on the market in series production. Its many advantages, such as emitting area light unlike LEDs, the lack of need for backlighting unlike LCDs, and the greater possible luminance (brightness) compared with EL film, have meant that this technology has made steps to establish itself in numerous areas, on the one hand as a replacement for conventional electroluminescent products and on the other in the development of new applications.

In the consumer sector in particular, suitable displays are already on the market for small portable electronic devices like MP3 players and mobile telephones. With reference to larger display dimensions, a Japanese manufacturer has already introduced the first device with a 40 inch (diagonal) screen to the public, but it will still require some years of development work before it is ready for the market and has a consumer-friendly price tag.

In 2005, as a result of cooperation between two German companies in the automobile sector, a small lighting unit for use in automobiles was presented at the international automobile exhibition in Frankfurt (IAA).

The following products with organic light-emitting diodes (OLED) are of current and future interest to architecture:

NON-FLEXIBLE OLED DISPLAYS
Available as SMOLEDs and POLEDs. Glass is one of the materials that can be used as a substrate. They can be applied to smooth surfaces, in housings etc., either attached mechanically or by adhesive and are currently available in 0.9, 1.2 and 1.6 inch diagonal sizes.
+ Market presence, can be used in low to medium temperature ranges (< –20°C to > +80°C), driven by low voltages, relatively low power consumption, dimmable, limited UV light resistance, smooth and flicker-free luminous surface, relatively large viewing angle (e.g. 160°), limited impact resistance, very short reaction times.
– Relatively sensitive to moisture, varying durability of pigment, relatively short life compared with LCD displays, no illumination of the edge of the display, therefore an edge cover is required, cannot be bent.

Technology by Novaled: white-light-emitting SMOLED display. | Coloured-light-emitting SMOLED displays. | Technology by Osram Opto Semiconductors: coloured-light-emitting POLED displays.

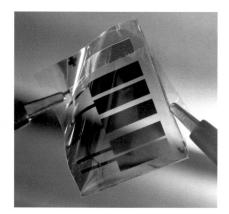

FLEXIBLE OLED DISPLAYS (E.G. TECHNOLOGY BY FRAUNHOFER INSTITUTE FOR APPLIED POLYMER RESEARCH)

Available as SMOLEDs and POLEDs. Polyethylene terephthalate (PET) is one of the materials that can be used as a substrate.

➕ Can be attached mechanically or by adhesive to curved or flexible substrates, e.g. three-dimensional curved membranes, unbreakable, otherwise as above.

➖ Lack of market presence, very small bevels or folds not possible; otherwise as above.

NON- AND SEMITRANSPARENT OLED LIGHT SOURCES (E.G. TECHNOLOGY BY OSRAM OPTO SEMICONDUCTORS)

Limited availability as SMOLEDs and POLEDs. Glass is one of the materials that can be used as a substrate. They can have their own housings, frames etc., therefore can stand alone or be attached mechanically or by adhesives to smooth substrates such as walls or ceilings. Light sources were developed as technology demonstrators, which were made up of several tiles (SMOLEDs) in a 2 inch x 3 inch (approx. 5 cm x 7.6 cm) format.

➕ As above.

➖ Lack of market presence, relatively short life (approx. 3000 hours), relatively low brightness (250 Cd/m², or 400 Cd/m² in future) compared with conventional light sources, edge cover required, cannot be bent or curved.

TRANSPARENT OLED LIGHT SOURCE (E.G. TECHNOLOGY BY NOVALED)

Technology demonstrators based on SMOLEDs. Glass is one of the materials that can be used as a substrate. They can have their own housings, frames etc., therefore can stand alone or be attached mechanically or by adhesives to smooth substrates such as walls or ceilings or into housings.

➕ Can be used in low to medium temperature ranges (< –20°C to > +80°C), relatively long replacement life (approx. 5000 to 200 000 hours, depending on the application), relatively high brightness possible (< 100 Cd/m² to > 5000 Cd/m², depending on the application).

➖ Lack of market presence, edge cover required, cannot be bent or curved, cannot be processed, e.g. cut, like conventional glass or EL films.

Currently available or developed products useful in architecture include:

RAW OR END PRODUCTS

Flexible displays using OLEDs (e.g. POLEDs)

Light sources (small) using OLEDs (e.g. SMOLEDs)

INTERMEDIATE OR END PRODUCTS

Light sources (large) using OLEDs (SMOLEDs)

Transparent light sources/day-night window using OLEDs (SMOLEDs)

Emergency lighting using OLEDs (SMOLEDs)

Several displays can be placed adjacent to one another to create large and/or curved surfaces. The non-luminous edge zones can result in unwanted blank areas. Temporary reduction of the output, e.g. by dimming the light, can increase the life of the display.

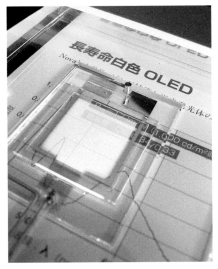

polymer/small molecule electroluminescence | organic light-emitting diodes (OLED) › projects

Due to the fact that currently few products incorporating organic light-emitting diodes (OLED) for use in architecture are available on the market, until now only a limited number of applications have been realised and given publicity. OLEDs are of particular interest as area light sources. Comparatively small light sources with uses such as emergency lighting are among the first products that will be available in the foreseeable future. Currently, development is taking place of a so-called day-night window based on small molecule technology, which allows natural sunlight to enter by day and serves as an artificial light source at night.

Technology by Osram Opto Semiconductors: technology demonstrator of an OLED light source consisting of two white-light-emitting tiles. | Technology by Novaled: technology demonstrator of a transparent OLED light source. | Weakly and strongly luminous examples. | *opposite:* Technology by Fraunhofer Institute for Applied Polymer Research: technology demonstrator of a flexible POLED display.

smartwrap

Polysmart materials | Polysmart application
Light-emitting and heat-storing smart materials:
**FILM WITH ORGANIC LIGHT-EMITTING DIODES (OLED), WITH
ORGANIC PHOTOVOLTAIC CELLS (OPV); FILM WITH PHASE CHANGE
MATERIALS (PCM)**

Kieran Timberlake Associates, USA
Pavilion with polyvalent building skin | Cooper Hewitt National Design
Museum, New York, USA (2003)

SmartWrap is the name of an innovative, polyvalent building skin which, on
the basis of a newly developed transfer technology, it is expected to open
up new possibilites for the industrial and cost-efficient use of smart materials in the future. In New York a pavilion was designed to demonstrate its
components and technology; this construction formed the main exhibition
piece of the August 2003 SOLOS exhibition at the Cooper Hewitt National
Design Museum.

SmartWrap was developed as a two-layer coating system by Kieran Timberlake Associates, an architectural practice based in Philadelphia, Pennsylva-
nia, in conjunction with students and partner companies. While the outside
layer forming the external facade skin consists of a transparent, elastic polyethylene terephthalate (PET), on which different electronic smart materials
can be applied by rolling and printing, the inside room-forming layer mainly
supports thermal insulation and heat storage materials.

SmartWrap will allow future building skins to appear on the market that will
have all the components required to convert and manage solar radiation. The
external skin is fitted with organic photovoltaic cells (OPV) to collect and
convert sunlight, with thin film batteries to store electrical energy, with conductive, printed circuits and organic thin film transistors (OTFT) for distrib-
uting the electricity and for controlling functions, with polymer-based OLEDs
for lighting and electronic displays, and with chromatic solar protection for
controlling the transmission of light and heat.

Adjacent to the outer skin there is a permanent thermally insulative layer of
air, which is formed with the help of the offset inner skin, in which are incorporated by means of pockets a thermally insulative aerogel and latent heat
storage, the latter in the form of phase change material (PCM).

In the pavilion only a small section of the building skin was fitted with the
innovative layer system. The larger part simulated the possible appearance
of *SmartWrap* using a printed PET film.

SmartWrap: view into the pavilion. | Preprinted roll machine. | View between the room-forming layer with PCM and facade-forming layer with OLEDs, thin film batteries and organic photovoltaic cells. | Building skin with *SmartWrap*, simulated with a printed PET film. | Night view.

electricity-generating smart materials

Electricity-generating smart materials include materials and products that are able to generate an electric current with a connected consumer (e.g. a resistance load) in response to one or more stimuli from outside influences, the effect of light, or changes in temperature and/or pressure.

The currently available electricity-generating smart materials can be differentiated according to their triggering stimuli as follows:

PHOTOELECTRIC SMART MATERIALS
After the connection of a consumer these materials generate an electric current when excited by the effect of light (electromagnetic energy).

THERMOELECTRIC (PYROELECTRIC) SMART MATERIALS
After the connection of a consumer these materials generate an electric current when excited by the effect of temperature (thermal energy).

PIEZOELECTRIC SMART MATERIALS
After the connection of a consumer these materials generate an electric current when excited by the effect of compression or tension (mechanical energy).

CHEMOELECTRIC SMART MATERIALS
After the connection of a consumer these materials generate an electric current when excited by the effect of a chemical environment (chemical energy).

Piezoelectric smart materials are inverse smart materials. They are able to generate electric charges from the effect of compression or tension, and in reverse change their shape on application of an electrical field. Both effects are discussed extensively in the following sections and hence they are omitted from the chapter on electroactive smart materials (pp. 66 ff.).

Chemical elements that for example consist of different noble metals and depend on the presence of an electrolyte such as salt water in order to generate an electric current are not classed as chemoelectric smart materials. As the less noble electrodes in these elements dissolve over time ("sacrificial electrodes"), they will not be dealt with any further here.

MATscape: detail of building skin with wind quills on the north side that are connected to piezoelectric cells.

PHOTOELECTRIC SMART MATERIALS >
MATERIALS, PRODUCTS, PROJECTS

Their inherent properties enable them to react to light (visible light, UV light; electromagnetic radiation) by generating an electric current with a connected consumer.

The following photoelectric smart materials are currently among those of interest to architects:

DYE SOLAR CELLS (DSC)

Other photoelectric smart materials include:

SILICON SOLAR CELLS

THIN FILM SOLAR CELLS

ORGANIC SOLAR CELLS (organic photovoltaics, OPV)

Silicon solar cells are based on comparatively old technology and are being increasingly superseded by new developments, such as thin film solar cells and organic solar cells. Information about new developments in silicon-based solar cells can be found on p. 41 f.

Depending on the dye used (e.g. anthocyanin), dye solar cells can also be classed as organic solar cells. They are based on a comparatively new technology in which the synthetic organic polymers, as light-sensitive components, are often interlayered between flexible substrate layers. They are currently in the market introduction phase (see p. 41 f.).

dye solar cells (DSC) › materials

Dye solar cells (DSC) are layer composites in which dyes among others are used as components that generate an electric current with a connected consumer by the absorption of light (electromagnetic radiation). They are also known as Grätzel cells (named after the Swiss developer of the basic technology), photo-electrochemical solar cells or nano solar cells (the latter name refers to the dimensions of the semiconductor component normally used, titanium dioxide TiO_2) (also see titanium dioxide (TiO_2), pp. 100 ff.).

In principle, DSCs consist of several functional layers placed one upon the other: a transparent anode, commonly tin oxide, is deposited on a supporting first substrate layer such as glass. A paste of TiO_2, perhaps only a few microns thick, is screen-printed and baked on top of the tin oxide to form a nanocrystalline semiconductor layer. After this comes the coating of the TiO_2, e.g. by dipping, with a light-absorbing dye, and an electrolyte layer, which may be an iodine solution, with a layer of e.g. platinum or graphite, which acts as a catalyst. The final layer is a substrate layer with a prefitted transparent electrode.

The development of the DSC goes back to the experiments by Michael Grätzel and his research team at the Federal Institute of Technology in Lausanne, Switzerland, at the beginning of the 1990s. In these experiments, dye and TiO_2 were tried in solar cells instead of silicon. Patenting followed in 1992. A number of research bodies have been working since then on optimising the technology. Efforts have concentrated mainly on the search for suitable, adequately cycle-stable dyes, the development of leakproof cells and on increasing the achievable effect. Apart from Switzerland, the leading research countries are Germany and Australia. An Australian company has just commenced series production of modules.

Materials and components generally used include among others:

INORGANIC AND ORGANIC DYES
Ruthenium complexes (e.g. N3, red dye, black dye), osmium complexes.
Organic dyes: anthocyanin (natural plant dyes, e.g. in hibiscus blossom and bilberry juice), bacterial chlorophylls (e.g. in purple bacteria)
Dye mixtures: porphyrins and phthalocyanines

The following material, or component respectively, is currently among those of interest in architecture:

Technology by Dyesol: screen-printed nanocrystalline TiO_2 layer. | Baking of TiO_2. | Introduction of dye into cells. | Technology by Fraunhofer Institute for Solar Energy Systems: optimisation and manufacture of pastes, colloids in the manufacture of DSCs.

RUTHENIUM COMPLEXES
Dyes based on the metallic element ruthenium and an organic solution.
+ Market presence, can be used in low to medium temperatures (< −20°C to > +80°C), very large number of absorption and emission cycles possible (up to about 50 million), much longer replacement life compared with e.g. anthocyanins.
− Relatively expensive compared with anthocyanins.

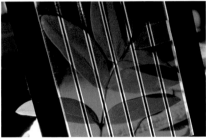

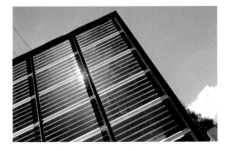

dye solar cells (DSC) › products

A number of different institutions are currently working on the optimisation of dye solar cells (DSCs). One aspect under investigation is the sealing of the edges of the cells, which is still a weak point. With a technology recently developed by the Fraunhofer Institute for Solar Energy Systems in Freiburg, Germany, the goal of long-term stability in excess of 10 years can now be achieved. This technology seals the modules with a glass solder to prevent leakage of liquid electrolyte and protect sensitive internal components from premature degradation. So far the technology is not yet ready for widespread market success, as its currently achievable efficiency is generally below 5% (in Japan an efficiency of 10.4% has been achieved on a 1 cm² surface) and an efficiency of about 12% can be obtained from today's silicon-based solar cells. In spite of this, international companies based for example in Australia are trying to establish DSC modules on the market albeit in small numbers; they aim especially at the German market, where the contribution of regenerative sources of electrical energy to the national grid is sub-sidised by the government.

DSCs are currently or likely to be available in the future as:

DSC MODULES (TECHNOLOGY BY DYESOL)
Several DSCs grouped into modules, with striped channels. They are available in individual housings, or housings or frames accommodating several modules (panels), which allow them to be stand-alone products or be attached mechanically or glued to flat surfaces, e.g. walls or roofs.
+ Market presence, generation of electric current with little light, can be used in low to medium temperatures (< –20°C to > +80°C), relatively long replacement life (approx. 500 to 5000 hours).
– Low efficiency (< 5% under standard testing conditions), cannot be bent or curved, cannot be handled like conventional glazing e.g. cut to shape, relatively expensive compared with modules of conventional silicon solar cells.

Technology by Dyesol: module of six DSCs. | Transparent effect of dye used. | Supported panel of several modules.

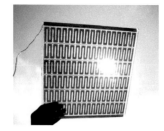

DSC MODULES (TECHNOLOGY BY FRAUNHOFER INSTITUTE FOR SOLAR ENERGY)

Technology demonstrators of DSCs comprising of several modules arranged together with meandering channels, sealed with screen-printed glass solder. They are available in individual housings or housings or frames accommodating several modules (panels), which allow them to be stand-alone units or be attached mechanically or glued to flat surfaces, e.g. walls or roofs. The maximum size of modules so far (technology demonstrators) is 30 cm x 30 cm, voltage approx. 4.2 V, current approx. 0.8 A.

+ Generation of electric current (electron-hole pairs) with low quantities of light, can be used in low to medium temperatures (< –20°C to > +80°C), edge areas have a long-lasting seal of glass solder, strength from the meandering bond pattern with the glass substrate.

– Lack of market presence, low efficiency (2.5%, may rise to 5% under standard testing conditions in future, depending on various aspects including printing techniques), transparency limited due to meandering bond pattern with the glass substrate, cannot be bent or curved, cannot be handled like conventional glazing e.g. cut to shape, relatively expensive compared with modules of conventional silicon solar cells.

The edge areas between the two glass substrates must not be allowed to leak, otherwise the long-term functionality of DSCs cannot be guaranteed. It is important to avoid excessive one-sided alternating thermal loads, such as arise with use as window glazing. This applies in particular to cells and modules with striped channels.

Products currently in use in architecture or likely to become relevant in future include:

RAW OR END PRODUCTS

DSCs (technologies by Dyesol and Fraunhofer Institute for Solar Energy Systems)

INTERMEDIATE OR END PRODUCTS

DSC modules (technologies by Dyesol and Fraunhofer Institute for Solar Energy Systems)

DSC panels (technologies by Dyesol and Fraunhofer Institute for Solar Energy Systems)

dye solar cells (DSC) › projects

Dye solar cells (DSC) can be generally attached like conventional silicon or thin film technology solar cells in front of facades and on building roofs or integrated into them. As long-term stability of up to 5000 hours (technology by Fraunhofer Institute for Solar Energy) is still relatively low at the moment, it would be prudent to ensure that the units can be easily disassembled for maintenance and repair and replaced. The edges should be protected against large mechanical and thermal loads, e.g. by thermal separation or offset frames.

The way DSCs work means that they are coloured and this makes them particularly interesting to the architect as formal or contrasting design objects in facades and roofs or, when dispensing with coloured filters, by integrating DSCs optically into similarly coloured roof areas.

The cells are transparent and hence can be used as glass components in facades and windows. The use of red dye without additional colour filters limits the scope of application as the admitted light, depending on the proportion and positioning of the active areas, will always be some shade of red. Another field of application is in areas that are permanently or temporarily subject to relatively small quantities of light (e.g. north-facing facades). Complicated adaptive tracking systems would then not have to be employed as often.

Up to now there have been only a few published implementations of DSCs in buildings.

Technology by Dyesol: building in Australia with DSC panels integrated into the external skin | *opposite:* Technology demonstrators by Fraunhofer Institute for Solar Energy Systems: single-colour module 30 cm x 30 cm composed of six DSCs. | Multicolour module, colours achieved by the use of photoactive, selective light-absorbent metal-organic complexes (dyes). | Module with printed graphic light-scattering layer (yellow area). All modules have a lasting seal based on a glass soldering technique developed at the Fraunhofer Institute for Solar Energy Systems.

THERMOELECTRIC SMART MATERIALS >
MATERIALS, PRODUCTS, PROJECTS

Their inherent properties allow them to react to temperature differences (temperature gradients) by absorbing heat (thermal energy) and generating an electric current with a connected consumer.

The following thermoelectric smart materials are currently of interest to architects:

THERMOELECTRIC GENERATORS (TEG)

Other thermoelectric smart materials are:

THERMOELEMENTS

RADIONUCLIDE BATTERIES

Thermoelements consist of pairs of wires of different metals, for example iron and copper-nickel, which are connected to one another at one point and by their generation of thermovoltages can be used to measure temperatures. They cannot generate large voltages and therefore are generally not suitable for use as sources of electric current.

Radionuclide batteries are thermoelectric generators that can generate thermovoltages by absorption of the decay heat from radioactive isotopes. Their uses include space travel among others.

thermoelectric generators (TEG) › materials

Thermoelectric generators (TEG), also known as thermogenerators, consist of thermoelectric components mainly made from highly doped p- and n-conducting semiconductors, less often from two wires of different metals, which accelerate electrons or generate electron-hole pairs by absorbing heat (thermal energy) in reaction to a temperature gradient.

Depending on their functional and constructional principles TEGs can be differentiated as p- and n-conducting semiconductors:

THERMOCOUPLE-BASED TEG
These are TEGs that consist of semiconducting, normally block-forming thermocouples produced by doping with different foreign atoms.
They are electrically in series and thermally in parallel to increase output. TEGs function as electron pumps. Manufacturing technology provides the market with thin film TEGs (thickness of semiconductor layers < 100 µm), thick film TEGs and macro-TEGs.

ELEMENT-BASED TEG
A relatively new development in which the TEGs consist of differently doped, semiconducting, stripe-forming elements. Their functional principle is similar to the solar cell. They therefore act as electron-hole pair generators. They can be classified as thin film TEGs, thick film TEGs or macro-TEGs, depending on the thickness of the semiconductor film.

The development of TEGs goes back to Thomas Johann Seebeck and the Seebeck effect named after him. In 1821 he discovered that a closed circuit of two wires of different metals produces a magnetic field due to the voltage they create when a temperature difference exists between the two contact points. In 1834 Jean Peltier discovered the reverse effect named after him: the creation of a temperature difference from an electric current. In the 1920s new semiconductor materials were developed that were used in TEGs. In the 1950s Abram Fedorovich Ioffe and his colleagues developed the concept of thermoelectric conversion on which today's theories are founded. By around 1960 a great number of semiconductor materials were being examined for their suitability in TEGs, including bismuth telluride, which is still in use today. Among the first users were NASA and the military. Today the search is for TEGs that can use the waste heat from combustion processes or solar radiation. In 2004 a new technology was introduced in which silicon was used as the semiconductor material to generate, similar to a solar cell, electric current by forming electron-hole pairs.

Materials and components in use for thermocouple-based TEGs include the following:

DOPED INORGANIC SEMICONDUCTORS
Bismuth telluride (Bi_2Te_3), iron disilicide ($FeSi_2$), silicon-germanium (SiGe), cobaltate ceramics.

GRADED DOPED INORGANIC SEMICONDUCTORS
Bismuth telluride/iron disilicide ($Bi_2Te_3/FeSi_2$)

DOPED INORGANIC SEMICONDUCTORS
Silicon germanium (SiGe).

The following materials and components are relevant for architectural uses or could be in the future:

BISMUTH TELLURIDE (BI_2TE_3)
Inorganic semiconductor alloy of metallic bismuth and metallic telluride (with gold- or silver-doped tellurium). This alloy can be further processed into p- and n-conducting semiconductors by doping with different foreign atoms. It is used in thermocouple-based and element-based TEGs.
Market presence, can be used in low to medium temperatures (> +300°C), good efficiency (approx. 8%, depending on temperature difference among other parameters).
Cannot be used in strongly oxidising atmospheres (e.g. gas burners).

IRON DISILICIDE ($FeSi_2$)
Inorganic semiconductor alloy composed of metallic iron and metallic silicon. This alloy can be further processed into p- and n-conducting semiconductors by doping with different foreign atoms. Is used for thermocouple-based TEGs.
+ Market presence, can be used in low and high temperatures (< +800°C), can be used in strongly oxidising atmospheres (e.g. gas burners).
− Low efficiency (approx. 3%, depending on temperature difference among other parameters), relatively expensive.

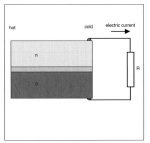

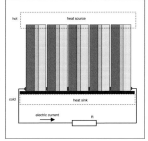

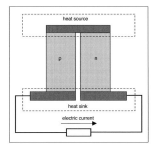

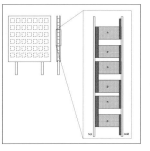

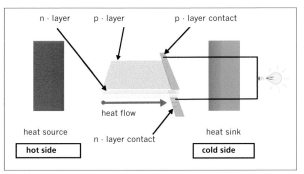

Schematic representation of construction and functioning of a thermocouple-based TEG (e.g. technology by Micropelt) and an element-based TEG (technology by SAM).

SILICON GERMANIUM (SiGe)
Inorganic semiconductor alloy composed of purified metallurgical grade silicon and germanium. This alloy can be further processed into p- and n-conducting semiconductors by doping with different foreign atoms. As well as in solar cells, it will also find future use in element-based TEGs.
⊞ Market presence, can be used in low and high temperatures (< +500°C), very good efficiency (> 15%, depending on temperature difference among other parameters), can be used in strongly oxidising atmospheres (e.g. gas burners).
⊟ Must be processed in purer form than e.g. bismuth telluride.

thermoelectric generators (TEG) › products

Although reversibly operable, thermoelectric generators (TEG) are different to Peltier elements (PE) or modules (PM). For example, the semiconductor alloys can be doped with various foreign atoms. Solder cannot be used in contact with heat sources at a temperature of more than 250°C. These are temperatures typically obtained by concentrating solar radiation by the use of prepositioned lenses. In certain situations there may be higher numbers of thermocouples in TEGs than in PEs. The reason that TEGs have been nowhere near successful on the market is their lower efficiency, which is quoted as between 3% to 4% (in contrast to efficiencies of more than 12% with conventional technologies).

Manufacturers of TEGs have generally concentrated on one of the above technologies. While some manufacturers offer very small, maximum size 5mm x 5mm, thin film technology TEGs with only a small electrical output of a few 100 µW that generate less than 100 mV voltage from relatively small temperature differences, other manufacturers concentrate on larger and more powerful TEGs and offer modules with electrical outputs rated at between 2.5 W to 19 W from relatively large temperature differences of up to several 100 K.

There are no known TEGs that have been developed specially for use in architecture and have reached market readiness. Universities in the USA and Europe are working on the development and testing of facade systems with PEs or PMs for active climatisation of rooms.

Bismuth crystal. | Tellurium crystal. |
Polycrystalline solar grade silicon.

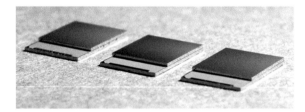

A development in the field of textiles from 2002 could be transferred to find applications in architecture. Integrable into fabrics, silicon thermogenerator chips have been developed to provide a battery-free electricity supply to various consumers incorporated into textile clothing. They use the small temperature difference between the inside and outside of the textiles to generate typical power outputs of approx. 1.0 mW and no-load voltages of approx. 10 V/cm² from a temperature difference of 5 K (in: [13]).

The use of TEGs to generate electric current is not new, but so far this technology has not been able to succeed in the market due to its low efficiency. In addition to optimising semiconductors, e.g. by grading different materials, developers have also sought to establish new silicon-based technologies. As efficiency depends on the size of the temperature difference, the products are used either in the heat given off by combustion processes or in concentrated solar radiation. The latter application is of special interest in architecture.

The following TEGs are either currently or likely to be available in the future and of use in the field of architecture:

MODULES OF THERMOCOUPLE-BASED, MICROSCALE TEG **(E.G. TECHNOLOGY BY MICROPELT)**
Several thermocouples of block-forming, less than 100 μm thick semiconductors (thin film TEGs) grouped into modules. These products can be fastened to smooth and flexible substrates, e.g. glass or membranes, either mechanically or by adhesive. The maximum size of the modules manufactured to date is 5 mm x 5 mm, their electrical output is less than 600 μW, voltage below 100 mV, current less than 40 mA, from a temperature difference of less than 20 K. A technology demonstrator currently being developed has given an electric output of 0.045 W, a voltage of 2.1 V and a current of 0.075 A from a temperature difference of 33 K. They can be used to provide an independent energy supply or energy support to sensors and other microsystems.
+ Market presence, generation of electric current from small temperature differences, can be used in low to medium temperatures (< +250°C hot sides), relatively long replacement life (approx. 100 000 hours, comparable with silicon solar cells).
− Low efficiency (< 5%, depending on the module and temperature), cannot be bent or curved.

Technology by Micropelt: schematic representation of the construction of a microscale TEG. | Three microscale TEGs.

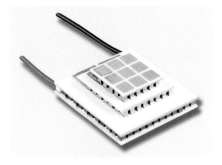

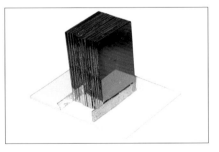

MODULES OF THERMOCOUPLE-BASED, MACROSCALE TEG (E.G. TECHNOLOGY BY HI-Z)

Several thermocouples of block-forming semiconductors less than 100 µm thick (thin film TEGs) grouped into modules. These products can be fastened to smooth and flexible substrates, e.g. glass or membranes, either mechanically or by adhesive. Up to now with a maximum size of 75 mm x 75 mm, the modules are capable of generating an electrical output of 19 W, a voltage of 5 V, a current of 8 A, from a temperature difference of 200 K. They can be used to provide an independent energy supply or energy support to sensors or other macrosystems and as a universally usable source of electricity.

+ Market presence, generation of electric current from small temperature differences, can be used in low to medium temperatures (< +230°C, hot sides), relatively long replacement life (approx. 500 to 5000 hours).

– Low efficiency (4.5 %, depending on the module and temperature), cannot be bent or curved, relatively expensive (approx. 154 US $/HZ-20 module, technology by Hi-Z).

MODULES OF ELEMENT-BASED, MACROSCALE TEG (TECHNOLOGY BY SAM)

Several elements of band-forming semiconductors (thin or thick film TEGs) grouped into modules. These products can be fastened to smooth and flexible substrates, e.g. glass or membranes, either mechanically or by adhesive. Up to now with a maximum size of 20 mm x 25 mm x 30 mm, the modules are capable of generating a voltage of approx. 2 V, a current of approx. 8 A, from a temperature difference of approx. 400 K. They can be used to provide an independent energy supply or energy support to sensors or micro/macrosystems and as a universally usable source of electricity.

+ Generation of electric current (electron-hole pairs) from small temperature differences, can be used in low to very high temperatures (in future < +1500°C hot side, component-dependent), in future very good efficiency (up to approx. 30 %, depending on module and temperature), in future very long replacement life (> 100 000 hours, comparable with silicon solar cells), in future relatively inexpensive (approx. < 1 euro/W).

– Lack of market presence, cannot be bent or curved.

Technology by Micropelt: illustration of PE. | Technology SCTB NORD: thermoelectric module. | Technology by FerroTec: special constructional form of PEs. | Technology demonstrators by SAM: module made up of a layered block of elements. | *opposite:* PM-based air conditioning system integrated into a building in 1958, designed by the RCA research department. | Refrigerator with PMs, around 1958.

In order to ensure the long-term functionality of TEGs they must not be subjected to temperatures above those specified for the particular product. In addition the electrical connections must not be broken or damaged, e.g. by mechanical loads such that they are reduced in cross section. Direct contact with water, moist and/or corrosive media must be prevented.

thermoelectric generators (TEG) › projects

At the moment there are no known applications of thermoelectric generators (TEG) to generate electric current in building envelopes. Current research mainly in the USA and Europe is examining the use of the Peltier effect in building envelopes to climatise rooms by active cooling and heating processes. That this idea is not new is shown by the earlier development at the end of the 1950s from the American company RCA, who, with Bell Telephone and Westinghouse, worked on a number of applications for "thermionic converters" and in 1958 demonstrated a suitably equipped electronic, vibration-free air conditioning system for buildings, which was the first of its kind at that time. Around that time RCA developed a refrigerator with the same technology.

Current researchers are seeking to integrate Peltier elements (PE) in multilayer systems for building envelopes, e.g. as active climatisation components in greenhouses, encapsulated between two conventional glass panes. Suitably configured, they could independently generate electric current for active cooling when temperatures rise too high inside the glazed building.

A more complex development that uses PEs with two hot sides comes from the USA. In the two skin system, the inner skin actively climatises the rooms with its flat, two-sided, active heatable PEs, while the outside skin generates the required electric current from its flat arrangement of photovoltaic elements.

If the costs drop in future below 1 euro/watt as predicted, TEGs could also find use in building envelopes, for example by the integration of suitable converters in textile membrane skins for residential and leisure buildings. This could be achieved in the first instance by weaving a membrane in a conventional way incorporating electrically conductive threads, then coating it with PVC and finally passing it through an automatic production line to produce individual TEG modules in a preset pattern to create electrical contact.

Products currently in use in architecture or likely to be relevant in future include:

RAW OR END PRODUCTS

THERMOCOUPLES for the manufacture of microscale TEGs (e.g. technology by Micropelt)

THERMOCOUPLES for the manufacture of macroscale TEGs (e.g. technology by Hi-Z)

ELEMENTS for the manufacture of macroscale TEGs (technology by SAM)

INTERMEDIATE OR END PRODUCTS

MODULES of thermocouple-based, microscale TEGs (e.g. technology by Micropelt)

MODULES of thermocouple-based, macroscale TEGs (e.g. technology by Hi-Z)

MODULES of element-based, macroscale TEGs (technology by SAM)

PIEZOELECTRIC SMART MATERIALS > MATERIALS, PRODUCTS, PROJECTS

These types of smart materials have inherent properties that enable them to generate electric charges when deformed by mechanical effects, e.g. compression.

The following piezoelectric smart materials are currently of interest to architects:

PIEZOELECTRIC CERAMICS (PEC)

PIEZOELECTRIC POLYMERS (PEP)

Other piezoelectric smart materials are:

PIEZOELECTRIC MONOCRYSTALS

Piezoelectric monocrystals include, for example, natural quartz crystals and tourmaline crystals, which have good piezoelectric properties but are only of secondary importance in their technical application. Crystals of sodium potassium tartrate found earlier use in the manufacture of sound pick-up cartridges. Today it is predominantly polycrystalline ceramics and polymers that are used, in particular for sensor and actuator technology.

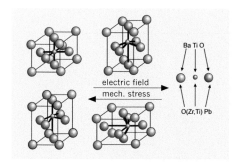

Schematic representation of the piezoelectric and inverse piezoelectric effect on the cubic and tetragonal structure of lead zirconate titanate (PZT) and barium titanate ($BaTiO_3$).

piezoelectric ceramics/polymers (PEC, PEP) › materials

Piezoelectric ceramics (PEC) and piezoelectric polymers (PEP), often referred to as piezoceramics and piezopolymers, are inorganic or organic materials that, when under a mechanical load, generate electric charges on their surfaces as a result of deformation through changes of charge distribution. In reverse, they can change their shape by the application of a voltage. These phenomena are described as the piezoelectric and the inverse piezoelectric effect respectively.

The piezoelectric effect was discovered in 1880 by the Curie brothers in natural Rochelle salt (or sodium potassium tartrate tetrahydrate, also known as Seignette salt), tourmaline and quartz crystals. They found that electrostatic charges result from mechanical loading of the crystal surfaces. These charges are proportional to the magnitude of the load. Among the first uses were ultrasound transducers and quartz resonators for frequency stabilisation. In 1950 a patent for a charge amplifier was granted to Walter P. Kistler, which helped ensure the widespread adoption of piezoelectric instrumentation technology. The first piezoelectric sensors were developed about ten years later. 1969 saw the discovery of the first highly active piezoelectric polymer materials. In the late 1990s a Finnish company developed a quasi-piezoelectric electret film, which is mainly used for sensors in a number of different applications.

Materials and components generally used as PECs include among others:

DOPED INORGANIC COMPOSITE CERAMICS
Lead zirconate titanate (PZT), lead magnesium niobate (PMN), barium titanate ($BaTiO_3$).

Materials and components generally used as PEPs include among others:

ORGANIC POLYMERS
Polyvinylidenfluoride (PVDF).

Materials and components generally used as QPEPs include among others:

ORGANIC ELECTRET POLYMERS
Polyolefines (polyethylene (PE), polypropylene (PP)).

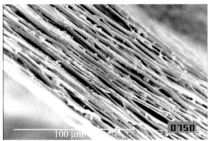

The following electrically charging materials and components are or could be important in the future in the field of architecture:

LEAD ZIRCONATE TITANATE (PZT)

Inorganic compound of lead (Pb), oxygen (O) and titanium (Ti) or zirconium (Zr). So-called hard and soft ceramics can be produced by doping with foreign atoms. Soft ceramics are more easily changed by electrical fields than hard ceramics. Their piezoelectric properties are the result of thermoelectric treatment by sintering and then polarisation under the influence of an electrical direct current field. One of its uses is for high voltage actuators.

+ Market presence, can be made in large quantities, many years of practical use, can be made to almost any shape, high stiffness, high dielectric constant, relatively inexpensive compared with PVDF.

− Sensitive to moisture, low tensile and shear capacity, toxic.

POLYVINYLIDENFLUORIDE (PVDF)

Semicrystalline thermoplastic plastic synthesised from hydrofluoric acid and methylchloroform. Its piezoelectric property is the result of mechanical-electric treatment by stretching and then polarisation under the influence of an electrical direct current field. Its uses include sensors.

+ Market presence, can be made in large quantities, highly elastic, non-toxic, insensitive to moisture, relatively inexpensive compared with PZT.

− Limited formability, low UV resistance.

POLYOLEFINES (POLYETHYLENE (PE), POLYPROPYLENE (PP))

Semicrystalline thermoplastic plastic synthesised from olefines such as ethylene or propylene in the presence of catalysts by polymerisation. Their quasi-piezoelectric properties are the result of electrical treatment by the permanent electrostatic charging of gas bubbles previously injected under high pressure. Their uses include sensors among others.

+ Market presence, can be made in large quantities, highly elastic, non-toxic, insensitive to moisture.

− Can only be used in low temperatures (−20°C to +50°C), limited formability, low UV resistance, relatively expensive compared with PZT.

SEM photograph of the crystal structure of barium titanate (BaTiO₃), colour digitally enhanced. | Various piezoceramic powders. | SEM photograph of multilayer polyolefin-based electret film.

piezoelectric ceramics/polymers (PEC, PEP) › products

Piezoelectric ceramics (PEC) and piezoelectric polymers (PEP) can generate electric charges under the effect of mechanical loads and the resulting deformations; they can also generate deformations under the effect of electrical fields. While the piezoelectric effect is mainly of use in sensor technology, the inverse piezoelectric effect is used primarily for actuators.

Ceramics and polymers have been only used to a secondary extent as piezoelectric generators because the obtainable power and current from the currently available products are very low in comparison with solar cells. While large, internationally active manufacturers of piezoceramic materials and products have developed and brought on to the market none or very few of their own generators, a few specialist companies have concentrated on the development and marketing of generators of various sizes for use in energy-independent micro- and macroscale systems in the field of sensor technology. Some of these products were developed for use in architecture, e.g. to provide an independent electricity supply to remote control sensors in switches. Foils have been developed for use under the walking surfaces of floors, which can indicate the load on the floor from the changes in charge caused by people walking on it.

In principle, actuators made from piezoceramic materials can also be used as generators. So-called bender actuators are very suitable for this as they can have relatively large travel distances compared with linear actuators. They are of interest to architects because they can be used in a relatively simple way to generate electric charges from building vibrations caused by the wind or the movement of people.

Technology by PI Ceramic: various multilayer bender actuators with connection wires, microprocessor to equalise sizes. | Various multilayer bender actuators with integrated positioning sensors. | Various multilayer linear actuators with ceramic insulation. | Various prestressed multilayer linear actuators, some fitted with connection wires. | CFP structure with integrated multilayer linear actuators (PICA actuator).

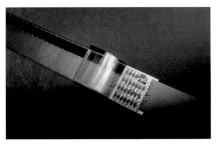

Technology by Mirow: various polymer film sensors (pressure converters) made from piezoelectric PVDF films: piezosensor array for flow analysis. | Seven piezosensors arranged adjacent to one another on transparent plastic support. | Sensor band for measuring pulse rates. | 50 bending sensor array for crash tests.

The following products based on PECs and PEPs are among those currently or likely to be available in the future and of use in architecture:

MULTILAYER BENDER ACTUATORS MADE FROM LEAD ZIRCONATE TITANATE (PZT) (E.G. TECHNOLOGY BY PI CERAMIC)

Linear monolithic bender actuators made from approx. 50 µm thick piezoceramic layers with internal silver palladium electrodes and ceramic insulation. They can be clamped at one or both ends depending on the shape and design. They can be used for example as piezoelectric generators, energy-independent sensors (piezoelectric effect) and for micropositioning and vibration absorption (inverse piezoelectric effect) on micro- and macroscale systems.

+ Market presence, can be used in low to medium temperatures (< +250°C, dependent on PZT modification among other parameters), relatively large travel distances achievable compared with multilayer linear actuators (> 2 mm, dependent upon dimensions and voltages among other parameters), with ceramic insulation largely insensitive to moisture, very long replacement life (> 1000000 cycles). Otherwise as for PZT above.

– Generates relatively small voltages (< ±30V), deformations must be within the permissible limits, i.e. max. 10% in excess of the actuator's travel distance, relatively low actuating force achievable compared with multilayer linear actuators.

MULTILAYER LINEAR ACTUATORS (STACK TRANSLATORS, LINEAR CONVERTERS) MADE FROM LEAD ZIRCONATE TITANATE (PZT) (E.G. TECHNOLOGY BY PI CERAMIC)

Linear converters made from e.g. approx. 25 µm to 100 µm thick block- or disc-shaped, stacked piezoceramic layers with internal electrodes, which are sintered together to form a monolith. They can be attached mechanically on flat surfaces, e.g. by clamping, or by gluing the top or bottom pieces of the unit in place. They can be used as piezoelectric generators, energy-independent sensors (piezoelectric effect) and for micropositioning and vibration absorption (inverse piezoelectric effect) on micro- and macroscale systems.

+ Market presence, can be used in medium temperatures (< +250°C, dependent on PZT modification among other parameters), very long replacement life (> 1000000 cycles), with ceramic insulation largely insensitive to moisture. Otherwise as for PZT above.

– Generates relatively small voltages (< ±30V), deformations must be within the permissible limits, i.e. max. 10% in excess of the actuator's travel distance, relatively short travel distance achievable compared with multilayer linear actuators (< 200 µm, dependent upon dimensions and voltages among other parameters).

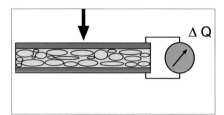

Osther constructional forms of actuators based on PECs are:

LAMINAR ACTUATORS (CONTRACTION ACTUATORS)
TUBE ACTUATORS (TUBES)
SHEAR ACTUATORS
PIEZOMECHANICS WITH INTEGRATED LEVER RATIO SETTING
PIEZO STAGES

POLYMER FILM SENSORS (PRESSURE CONVERTERS) MADE FROM POLYVINYLIDENFLUO-RIDE (PVDF) (E.G. TECHNOLOGY BY MIROW)
Flat composites made from single- or multiple-layered transparent film layers (films) of polyvinylidenfluoride (PVDF), with thin electrically conductive coatings on both sides, e.g. of vapour-deposited metals, surrounded by metal films or conductive plastic films, which act as electrodes. Other protective coatings could be added, for example PET. Available in different sizes. They can be attached to flat, round and flexible substrates by mechanical fixings or by gluing. They can be used as energy-independent sensors (piezoelectric effect) and for deforming (inverse piezoelectric effect) on micro- and macroscale components or systems.
✚ Market presence, long replacement life (> 1 000 000 cycles), high compressive strength, insensitive to impact, can be cut to shape, can be bent (depending on the electrodes used). Otherwise as for PVDF above.
▬ Only relatively low to medium voltages can be generated (< ±200 V/µm); deformations must be within the permissible limits. Otherwise as for PVDF above.

ELECTRET POLYMER FILM SENSORS (PRESSURE CONVERTERS) MADE FROM POLYOLE-FINES (E.G. TECHNOLOGY BY EMFIT)
Flat composites made from multiple layers of polyolefine-based film with embedded, electrostatically charged gas bubbles, both sides are enclosed in thin aluminium foil, which act as the electrodes. Other protective coatings could be added, for example PET. Available in different shapes and sizes, for example as 580 mm wide rolls. These products can be fastened to smooth and flexible substrates, e.g. on or under floor coverings, on seating or beds, either mechanically or by adhesive. They can be used as energy-independent sensors (quasi-piezoelectric effect). To amplify their output they can be placed in series with voltage or charge amplifiers, or with so-called control units, which at the moment require a separate power supply, for optical or acoustic indication.
✚ Market presence, long replacement life (> 1 000 000 cycles), high compressive strength, insensitive to impact, can be cut to shape. Otherwise as for polyolefines above.
▬ Only relatively low to medium voltages can be generated (< ±200 V/µm); deformations must be within the permissible limits, cannot be bent. Otherwise as for polyolefines above.

Technology by Emfit: schematic representation of the construction and functioning of an electret polymer film sensor. | Rolled-up electret polymer film sensor with connection lead for connection to a control unit. | Technology by EnOcean: piezo radio transmitter module PTM 100 with rocker model.

In order to ensure the long-term functionality of products based on PECs and PEPs, they must not be subjected to mechanical or electrical loads in excess of those specified for the particular product. In addition the electrical connections must not be broken or damaged by mechanical loads with the result that they are reduced in cross section. Direct contact with moist and/or corrosive media is detrimental to PECs even with insulation and hence is to be prevented.

Products currently in use in architecture or likely to become relevant in future include:

RAW OR END PRODUCTS:

MULTILAYER BENDER ACTUATORS made from or incorporating lead zirconate titanate (PZT) (e.g. technology by PI Ceramic)

MULTILAYER LINEAR ACTUATORS (stack translators, linear converters) made from or incorporating PZT (e.g. technology by PI Ceramic)

LAMINAR ACTUATORS (contraction actuators) made from or incorporating PZT (e.g. technology by PI Ceramic)

TUBE ACTUATORS (tubes) made from or incorporating PZT (e.g. technology by PI Ceramic)

SHEAR ACTUATORS made from or incorporating PZT (e.g. technology by PI Ceramic)

PIEZOMECHANICS with integrated lever ratio setting made from or incorporating PZT (e.g. technology by PI Ceramic)

PIEZO STAGES made from or incorporating PZT (e.g. technology by PI Ceramic)

POLYMER FILM SENSOR (pressure converter) made from polyvinylidenfluoride (PVDF) (e.g. technology by Mirow)

ELECTRET POLYMER FILM SENSOR (pressure converter) made from polyolefines (e.g. technology by Emfit)

CFRP structure with e.g. integrated multilayer linear actuators (stack translators, linear converters) incorporating PZT (e.g. technology by PI Ceramic)

PIEZO RADIO TRANSMITTER MODULE (technology by EnOcean)

FLOOR with electret POLYMER FILM SENSOR (pressure converter) made from POLYOLEFINES (e.g. technology by Emfit)

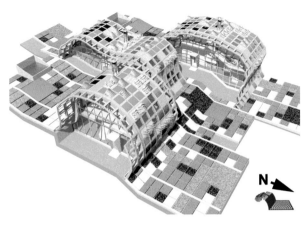

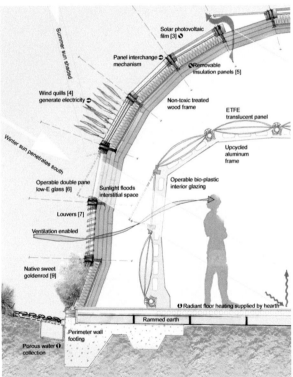

piezoelectric ceramics/polymers (PEC, PEP) › projects

The use of bender actuators in the field of architecture is currently being studied at numerous universities. In 1998 for example, the German Research Foundation (DFG), formed a special research group 409 for adaptive structures in aircraft and lightweight construction to investigate their use in other applications; by now this group has completed its work. An important aspect is the use of components incorporating piezoelectric materials for active sound reduction and for vibration absorption in building components. In these areas there has been cooperation with other research groups in the fields of air and space travel and materials science, among others.

As well as the use of inverse piezoelectric effects, there are also some applications for products that exploit the piezoelectric effect. For example, the aviva MUNICH building in Munich's commercial district has remote-controlled, batteryless, piezo radio switches for operating the Venetian blinds and lighting in the office rooms. Radio technology allows wiring and flush-mounted boxes to be dispensed with. Internal wall arrangements are more flexible and walls can be moved relatively inexpensively.

The use of electret polymer film sensors also opens up some interesting possibilities. One of the uses for these extremely pressure-sensitive and very thin sensors is for installation under floor coverings. In Finland in 2005 the floors of two detainment cells in a small police station were fitted with these devices as an experiment. The sensors were placed between the concrete floor surface and the linoleum floor covering. If the police station is unmanned and prisoners escape from the cells, the system alerts a neighbouring station over a digital mobile phone network. In Japan the Kaimin System, intended for use in "intelligent rooms" and fully equipped with sensors, was developed. The system used polymer film sensors as sleep sensors in bed heads.

Building with solar cells (south side) and wind quills (north side) connected to piezoelectric cells: *MATscape*, Mitchell Joachim, Lara Greden, Whitney Jade Foutz, Wendy Meguro, Luis Rafael Berrios-Negron (2005).

How Light is changed into sound

> Monosmart material | Monosmart application
> Electricity-generating, shape-changing smart materials:
> **BALSAWOOD BOARDS AND STONES WITH PEC ELEMENTS (LINEAR ACTUATORS)**
> Sound installation controlled by light and hardware

Felix Hess, Netherlands
Sound installation | Warsaw Autumn, Centre for Contemporary Art, Warsaw, Poland (1996)

How Light Is Changed Into Sound is the name for a series of interactive sound installations of the Dutch artist Felix Hess. The research physicist developed small electronic sound machines (described by him as "cracklers"), which react to changes in air pressure and brightness with sporadic, irregular clicking noises; the hearer associates these sounds with the croaking of frogs.

Each of these sound machines consists of a small circuit board on which the few required electronic components are soldered and connected by wires to a low voltage supply; the actual sound generator is connected to a power circuit. Whilst in the installation *It's in the Air* the circuit boards used to react to changes in air pressure were additionally equipped with sound sensors and a conventional 9 volt block-battery, for his installation *How Light Is Changed Into Sound* the artist used small solar panels.

In both cases the sound generator consists of a wired piezo element, which works in conjunction with a small stone and a balsawood sounding board on its underside to amplify the sound. The electric current generated and flowing through the piezo element deforms it in a semi-rhythmic manner and excites the sounding board to vibrate.

For his installation *How Light Is Changed Into Sound* at the Warsaw Autumn cultural festival, the artist set up four such sound generators on the floor in one half of a room, spaced apart and connected together by a central circuit board. In addition to the circuit board, each sound generator was connected to four small solar panels on each side. Sunlight entered in various qualities through three window openings. Depending on the transient dynamic variations in brightness in the room and the number and changes in position of observers, the solar panels generated varying amounts of current which enlivened the inconspicuous room with irregular clicking noises.

How Light Is Changed Into Sound: view into the installation room with its four "Cracklers". | Close-up photograph of a sound generator for the installation *It´s in the Air.*

Dynaflex p01

Monosmart materials | Polysmart application
Colour- and optically changing smart materials:
GLASS WITH ELECTROOPTIC COATINGS
Electricity-generating smart materials:
**BENDER ACTUATORS WITH PIEZOCERAMIC MADE
FROM PZT**
A construction that dynamically changes its light
transmission properties in response to live loads and
mechanical vibrations

Axel Ritter, Germany
**Weight-controlled pavilion with optically changing
building envelope** | Germany (1995)

Dynaflex p01 is a reactive, mechanical structure, capable
of carrying foot traffic, which reacts to changing internal live
loads with expansions and deformations and can be called
a biomechanoid.

The construction is intended to be a pavilion and is almost
completely composed of glass fibre reinforced plastic. It
consists of seven modules of elliptical cross section. Each
module has an outside ring and two adjacent inner rings,
which are attached to one another at the sides at the vertices
of the ellipse. The outer and inner rings are supported at the
floor by a traverse with spring bearings by means of two
pairs of struts, with the inner ring having two bases resting
on the floor.

Each traverse carries a vertically moving load distribution
plate. When loaded, the traverse moves to the right, left or
slightly downwards. This causes the cross section of the
outer ring to become more circular and the connected strut
pairs press the inner rings apart: as a result the pavilion
changes in length depending on the deflection. In addition
to right, left and straight-ahead movements, the lateral connection nodes move up or down to affect the openings of two
neighbouring modules, which can change their positions in
any direction.

Dynaflex p01: demonstration model with supporting hairs
equipped with piezoelectric bender actuators and individually
attached electrooptic-/-chromic glass elements.

The external skin is formed of electrooptical glass elements. These elements are attached in rows to the outer ring and fastened on a crown of flexible supporting hairs with round cross sections and equipped with piezoelectric bender actuators. This ensures that the glass elements and the support hairs are not damaged on the relatively tightly curved surfaces.

Voltages are generated depending on the vibrations caused by wind or people, which in turn causes the electrooptical layers, via the connected electronic units, to change more or less dynamically from transparent to opaque. Thus the activities taking place can be discerned not only from the deformations but also from the glass elements of the external skin. In addition, it would be possible to display the critical loading states caused by the mechanical stresses. The loading states would be visualised in the colour changes of the glass elements of the corresponding electrochomic layers.

The principle of weight-controlled mechanical expansion as used here, and the potential expansions and deformations deriving from it, can be transferred to other types of building structures. A building designed with this principle could provide enhanced flexibility of use by temporarily claiming additional space. For example, in case of use as a kindergarten an additional interior space could be provided in the morning, which would then be available as a playground or car park during other parts of the day.

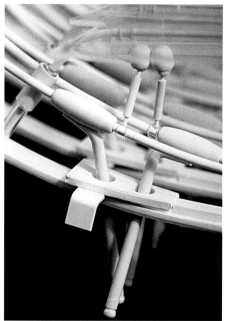
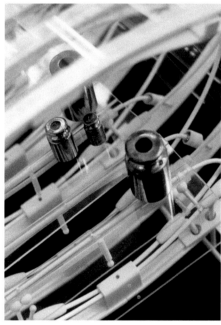

Dynaf | e x p01: Actuating cam for changing the geometry, inner and outer rings of a module, internal detail. | Load distribution plates with traverses pressing on the outside rings. | Connection of load distribution plate, strut pair inner and outer rings. | Internal detail.

energy-exchanging smart materials

Energy-exchanging smart materials, including energy-storing smart materials, are materials and products that are able to store energy, both sensible and latent energy, e.g. in the form of light, heat, electricity or hydrogen, and exhibit at least some reversibility.

The energy-storing smart materials available on today's market can be differentiated as follows:

LIGHT-STORING SMART MATERIALS
These materials have inherent properties that enable them to store energy in the form of light.
HEAT-STORING SMART MATERIALS
These materials have inherent properties that enable them to store energy in the form of heat and cold (negative heat).
ELECTRICITY-STORING SMART MATERIALS
These materials have inherent properties that enable them to store energy in the form of electricity.
HYDROGEN-STORING SMART MATERIALS
These materials have inherent properties that enable them to store energy in the form of hydrogen.

Heat-storing smart materials are discussed in the following section. Some light-emitting smart materials also have the ability to store light, and therefore light-storing smart materials are discussed in that section (see light-emitting smart materials, pp. 110 ff.). Electricity-storing smart materials are not sufficiently developed at the moment and there is little information available on them. A number of the systems for storing electricity in use today, for example lead accumulators, with their reduced capacity in cold conditions, have a degree of reversibility. However, for these products this reversibility is normally unwelcome. New developments in this area are seeking to eliminate much of this temperature dependency. Metal hydrates are particularly suitable for use as hydrogen-storing materials, but as they lack reversibility they cannot be classed as smart materials.

Technology by GLASSX: light-directing insulation glazing system with salt hydrate PCM; indoor view of installed unit.

HEAT-STORING SMART MATERIALS >
MATERIALS, PRODUCTS, PROJECTS

These materials have inherent properties that enable them to store energy in the form of heat and cold (negative heat) as latent energy.

The following latent heat-storing smart materials are currently of interest in the field of architecture:

PHASE CHANGE MATERIALS (PCM)

Other materials and products with relatively high heat-storing capacity and/or relatively low heat dissipation are usually not counted among smart materials and will not be discussed further here.

phase change materials (PCM) › materials

In principle, all materials that are able to reversibly change their state in response to external influences are classed as phase change materials (PCM). The type of influence or loading that instigates the change of phase is not important. Most of the known materials exhibit temperature-dependent phase changes. There are also other influences, e.g. chemical stimuli or the intake of matter, which can trigger phase changes and these are often associated with changes in elasticity. In addition to the states of solid, liquid and gas, there are other, largely stable intermediate states, such as the colloidal state derived from gels.

In the construction and architecture industries the term PCM has become generally applicable to materials and products that can be used as temperature-regulating media, for example latent heat or latent cold storage media for the regulation of temperatures. They have the property, below an inherent material-dependent phase change temperature, to change their state from liquid to solid by crystallisation and release a quantity of heat energy previously taken in and stored at a higher temperature. In the course of the phase change from solid to liquid and during the heat energy input the temperature of the material remains constant.

Among the first users of PCMs in the 1960s was NASA, who experimented with these materials and various applications in the field of space flight. Towards the end of the last century, the German Aerospace Center (DLR), developed a latent heat storage medium, based on sodium acetate and a heat transfer oil, for use in buildings. PCMs were used first in the USA, then later in other countries including Germany, in panels and other cladding components.

Materials and components in use include among others:

ORGANIC COMPOUNDS
Paraffins, paraffin mixtures (waxes).

INORGANIC COMPOUNDS
Salt hydrate, salt hydrate mixtures (eutectic mixtures), water, water mixture.

ORGANIC-INORGANIC COMPOUNDS
Paraffin-salt hydrate mixtures, water mixture.

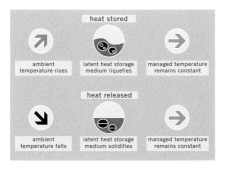

Schematic representation of the functioning of a latent heat storage medium.

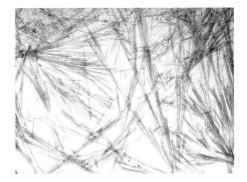

Microscopic-scale photograph of salt hydrate crystals. | Conventional close-up photograph of slightly heated salt hydrate (part of following photograph). | Conventional photograph of salt hydrate crystals.

Materials and components for the manufacture of PCMs must be able to function over a comparatively high number of charging and discharging cycles and, depending on the application, undergo relatively little change in volume. When used in building materials or components, direct contact points should be eliminated as far as possible to prevent structural damage. This can be achieved by encapsulation (micro-, macroencapsulation).

The following PCMs are among those of interest in architecture:

PARAFFINS, PARAFFIN MIXTURES
The melting temperature depends on the particular paraffin used and any added constituents.
➕ Market presence, can be made in large quantities, many years of practical use, can be used over a relatively large temperature range (approx. –12°C to +180°C), wide range of applications, insensitive to mechanical vibrations, maintenance-free, long replacement life.
➖ Highly combustible, volume change at phase change, relatively expensive compared with water-based PCMs and still expensive compared with salt hydrate-based PCMs.

SALT HYDRATE, SALT HYDRATE MIXTURES
The melting temperature depends on the particular salt hydrate used and any added constituents.
➕ Non-combustible, can be used over a relatively large temperature range (approx. –70°C to +120°C, including negative melting salt-water eutectics), relatively inexpensive compared with paraffin-based PCMs. Otherwise as above.
➖ Tendency to supercool when used for cold storage, tendency to segregate, volume change at phase change, tendency to promote corrosion.

WATER, WATER MIXTURE
The melting point of water is 0°C.
➕ Leaks are not hazardous to groundwater, can be used over a relatively large temperature range (approx. –40°C to +100°C), no tendency to segregate, relatively inexpensive compared with paraffin- and salt hydrate-based PCMs.
➖ Relatively poor thermal conductivity compared with paraffin- and salt hydrate-based PCMs, volume change at phase change.

SILICATE
Used in the form of powder as the carrier medium for embedding various PCMs, proportion of composite material approximately 40%.
➕ In powder form one of its suitable uses is for filling containers, relatively little volume change at phase change.
➖ None known.

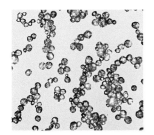

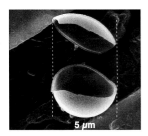
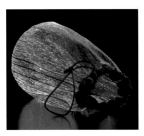

phase change materials (PCM) › products

Phase change materials (PCM) have a wide range of uses, for example in clothing textiles, in motor vehicles, as external panels and partitions, and in refrigeration and heating systems.

In recent years, a relatively large number of products for architecture have been developed and brought to the market. They are mainly used for passive climatisation of e.g. wall and ceiling components. Some more ambitious applications are now being tried following a phase of observation and testing in small projects.

Products are now available that can be used in existing and new buildings. Their solid walls enable many old buildings to buffer temperature peaks so that for example their rooms stay comfortably cool for longer in the summer months, but new buildings usually lack these thermal storage masses. Compact external walls with highly heat-insulative and heat-storing components can be constructed by the intelligent incorporation of latent heat-storing products based on PCMs, such as appropriately designed gypsum plasterboards, plaster or even complex facade systems. Existing buildings can be improved by increasing their storage mass by retrofitting PCM-containing products.

There are various raw, intermediate and end products on the market. These range from granulates to composite materials with graphite to complex light-directing insulation glazing systems with integral salt hydrate-filled plastic panels.

Of the products on the market incorporating PCMs the main interest in architecture for the foreseeable future is, among others, in products that store latent heat and regulate temperature:

MICROENCAPSULATED PCM (E.G. MICRONAL, TECHNOLOGY BY DASF)
Plastic-encapsulated paraffin-based PCMs for passive climatisation of e.g. internal walls and ceilings, available e.g. as a powder for incorporation into other construction materials such as plaster, chipboard and fillers.
+ Market presence, can be made in large quantities, can be incorporated into different construction materials, available as various end products such as PCM plaster, resistant to mechanical damage, e.g. cutting. Otherwise as above for paraffins, paraffin mixtures.
− Not universally available, only approved end products can be used, cannot be used alone because of inadequate fire resistance (fire safety). Otherwise as above for paraffins, paraffin mixtures.

Technology by DASF: microscopic-scale photograph of Micronal microcapsules with diameters of 2 μm to 20 μm. | Microscopic-scale photograph of an individual Micronal microcapsule. | Dispersion with Micronal microcapsules. | Plaster pattern with Micronal microcapsules. | Technology by Dörken: aluminium composite bag with salt hydrate filling.

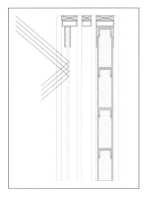

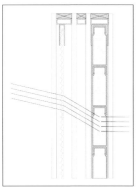

Technology by GLASSX: section through light-directing insulation glazing system with salt hydrate PCM. | Operating principle at high and low solar positions.

PLASTER WITH PCM (E.G. TECHNOLOGY BY DASF)

Include microencapsulated paraffin-based PCMs, for passive climatisation of internal walls and ceilings, can be handled and applied as conventional plaster.

+ Market presence, can be made in large quantities, can be coloured by the application of paint or the addition of pigments, easy to apply. Otherwise as above for paraffins, paraffin mixtures.

– Not universally available, relatively expensive compared with conventional plasters.

GYPSUM PLASTERBOARD WITH PCM (E.G. TECHNOLOGY BY DASF)

Currently available as 2000 mm x 1250 mm x 15 mm board, can be handled and fixed as conventional plasterboard or fibre-cement boards. Otherwise as above.

+ Thermal conductivity comparable with that of conventional plasterboard. Otherwise as above.

– Relatively expensive compared with conventional plasterboard. Otherwise as above.

ALUMINIUM FOIL BAGS WITH PCM (E.G. TECHNOLOGY BY DÖRKEN)

Aluminium foil bags with salt hydrates or salt hydrate mixtures for passive climatisation of e.g. ceilings will improve thermal conductivity if placed adjacent to components with good conductivity (e.g. made from metal) and can for example be applied to suspended ceilings.

+ Market presence, can be made in large quantities, as it is not solid it does not damage cladding materials, easy to apply. Otherwise as above for salt hydrate, salt hydrate mixtures.

– Overhead leaks are hazardous to health, may cause property damage, additional laminar components required.

LIGHT-DIRECTING INSULATION GLAZING SYSTEM WITH MACROENCAPSULATED PCM (TECHNOLOGY BY GLASSX)
Insulation glazing system consisting of four panes positioned one behind the other with external integrated light-directing prismatic plastic panels and internal integrated transparent plastic containers filled with salt hydrate. The system provides passive climatisation of the facade and can be used in almost the same way as conventional insulation glazing systems.
+ Market presence, can be made in large quantities, can be incorporated alongside conventional glazing allowing the detailing to be simple, relatively easy to install, can indicate charge state. Otherwise as above for salt hydrate, salt hydrate mixtures.
− Higher replacement cost of defective panes and PCM containers, relatively heavy with consequences for installation costs, high manufacturing and installation costs compared with conventional insulation glazing. Otherwise as above.

Currently available or developed products relevant to architecture include:

RAW OR END PRODUCTS:

POWDER e.g. microencapsulated PCMs (e.g. Micronal)

DISPERSION e.g. microencapsulated PCMs
(e.g. Micronal)

COMPOUNDS (granulate, panels) e.g. PCM/graphite, PCM/plastic

INTERMEDIATE OR END PRODUCTS:

PLASTER containing microencapsulated PCMs
(paraffin, e.g. Micronal)

FILLER containing microencapsulated PCMs
(paraffin, e.g. Micronal)

GYPSUM PLASTERBOARD containing microencapsulated PCMs (paraffin, e.g. Micronal)

ALUMINIUM FOIL BAGS filled with PCMs
(salt hydrate, salt hydrate mixtures)

LIGHT-DIRECTING INSULATION GLAZING SYSTEM with macroencapsulated PCMs (paraffin)

LIGHT-DIRECTING INSULATION GLAZING SYSTEM with macroencapsulated PCMs (salt hydrate)

phase change materials (PCM) › projects

A number of different products incorporating phase change materials (PCM) have been in use in architecture for several years now. Among the first applications in existing and new buildings were microencapsulated PCMs. In 2001 the internal walls of a low-energy building, a so-called 3-litre-house, in Ludwigshafen, Germany, were plastered with gypsum plaster containing micro-encapsulated PCM. To optimise temperature management in another building, one of Berlin's refurbished residential and office complexes on the Spree River, latent heat storage was incor-porated into the plaster of a chilled ceiling, using a capillary tube mat. In 2005 the classrooms of a high school in Lauffen am Neckar, Germany, were built using lightweight construction in which approx. 500 m^2 gypsum plasterboard panels incorporating microencapsulated paraffin-based PCM were used.

Macroencapsulated PCMs so far have only been used in new buildings. In 2000, architect Diet-rich Schwarz installed macroencapsulated PCM in the southern facade of a solar house in Ebnat-Kappel, Switzerland. In conjunction with a south German company, the Swiss architect developed a light-directing insulation glazing system with macroencapsulated paraffin as the PCM and used this for his innovative temperature-regulating facade. Due to the high inflamma-bility of the paraffin a comparable insulation glazing system was developed soon after, using salt hydrate held in transparent plastic containers; this glazing system was approved exclusively for use as a construction product. In 2004 a relatively large building complex with 20 senior citizens' apartments was built using this system, which is described briefly below.

Sonnenschiff, equipped with gypsum plasterboard panels with microencapsulated paraffin-based PCM.

senior citizens' apartments

Monosmart material | Monosmart application
Heat-storing smart material:
INSULATION GLASS WITH PCM (SALT HYDRATE)
Intelligent management of solar radiation

Dietrich Schwarz, Switzerland
Senior citizens' apartments with a latent heat-storing glass facade |
Domat/Ems, Switzerland (2004)

Swiss architect Dietrich Schwarz has shown in several of his buildings how, in addition to their latent heat-storing properties, the ability of PCMs to change their optical appearance can also be used in a facade. The initial solution involved pure paraffin in transparent hollow plastic blocks, used as latent heat storage facade elements in the south facade of a zero energy house in Ebnat-Kappel, Switzerland. In contrast, for this project a salt hydrate was used as the PCM, due to fire safety reasons.

On the south side of this complex the architect installed a new design of a latent heat-storing insulation glazing system filled with salt hydrate over an area of 148 m². Called GLASSXcrystal, the 78 mm wide system is constructed like an ordinary triple insulation glazing unit, but with a light-directing prism panel outside and a PCM panel inside, consisting of polycarbonate containers filled with a salt hydrate mixture, which stores heat at +26°C to +28°C.

In summer the solar radiation is reflected back outside by the prismatic panels. During the winter the lower sun angle allows the solar radiation to pass almost unimpeded into the facade construction, where it hits the PCM panel, is converted into thermal radiation and stored by the melting of the salt hydrate. If the room temperature falls below +26°C, perhaps at night or on cloudy days, the salt hydrate crystallises and releases its stored heat energy into the room.

The charge state of this latent heat-storing glass facade can be observed directly from its optical appearance, which is determined by the different phases of the salt hydrate: if the facade looks opaque (seen from outside through the prismatic panels or from the inside), then the salt hydrate is uncharged. If it appears translucent (seen from outside through the prismatic panels) or transparent (from the inside, with no printed pattern), the salt hydrate is being charged or is fully charged.

Senior citizens' apartments: view of south facade. | Side view of south facade. |
Inside view of latent heat-storing facade.

Senior citizens' apartments: outside detail of latent heat-storing facade, uncharged state (opaque). | Detail of latent heat-storing facade, charged state (translucent).

matter-exchanging smart materials

matter-exchanging smart materials

Matter-exchanging smart materials, including matter-storing smart materials, are materials and products that are able to reversibly take up and/or in, to bind and release matter either in the form of molecules, as gaseous, liquid or solid components by various physical and/or chemical processes.

The taking-up and -in of matter may be activated, among others, through hygroscopic surfaces, e.g. by embedding hydrophilic components in a shape-giving matrix; through electrostatic surfaces, e.g. by the creation of an ionised electrical field; or through magnetic surfaces, e.g. by the creation of an electromagnetic field. This is in contrast to conventional methods of storing matter, which are mainly based on mechanical principles. Examples of this would be containers and natural or synthetic sponges.

The matter-storing smart materials currently available on the market can be differentiated on the basis of the type of matter stored, which can also be the triggering stimulus:

GAS/WATER-STORING SMART MATERIALS
They are excited by gas and/or water to adsorb or absorb them. Through contact with another medium such as air, and in certain situations through other influences (e.g. increased temperatures), they can become excited and desorb the stored matter.
PARTICLE-STORING SMART MATERIALS
They are excited for example by ionised, electrical or electromagnetic fields to absorb particles. When the field is removed, they are excited and desorb the stored matter.

Materials and products that can become electrostatically charged as a result of a stimulus are also examples of particle-storing smart materials. Architects R&Sie... give an indication of how electrostatically charged surfaces could be incorporated into buildings with their design *Dusty Relief/B-mu*, a museum of the future for Bangkok.

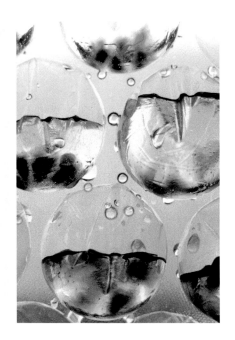

Hydroabsorber foils: detail of several cells with roughly half-swelled AP crystals.

The inherent properties of these materials allow them to react to the influence of gases and/or water in the form of water vapour, water or aqueous solutions by attaching them to their inner surfaces or taking them into their volume. Depending on the process involved, they may reversibly change their volume, density and optical properties and/or their energy state.

The storage may also involve a conversion of the matter taken up or the components, and through this a release of energy, for example as process heat from exothermic reactions, may take place. One or several stimuli such as the influence of a certain temperature, a particular chemical environment or the removal of an electrical field release the previously attached or embedded matter.

Depending on the mechanism of the taking-up of the components, the effect may be classed as adsorption and absorption. Adsorption describes the taking-up of an atom or molecule of a component on to an inner surface of a material or product, the adsorbent. Absorption describes the taking-in of an atom or molecule of a component into the volume of a material and/or product, the absorbent. The release or removal of a previously adsorbed or absorbed atom or molecule of a component is termed desorption (see adhesion-changing smart materials, pp. 98 ff.).

The following gas/water-storing smart materials are currently of interest to architects:

MINERAL AD-/ABSORBENTS (MAd, MAb)

ABSORBENT/SUPERABSORBENT POLYMERS (AP/SAP)

Other gas/water-storing smart materials include:

OTHER INORGANIC ADSORBENTS (IAd)

ORGANIC ADSORBENTS (OAd)

OTHER ORGANIC ABSORBENTS (OAb)

mineral ad-/absorbents (MAd, MAb) ›
materials

Mineral adsorbents (MAd) are materials or components with a liquid or solid phase that are able to take up gaseous components on to their inner surfaces and as a result reversibly change their volume, density, optical properties and/or their energy state. By contrast, mineral absorbents (MAb) are materials or components with a liquid or solid phase that are able to take up liquid components on their inner surfaces and take them into their volume and, where necessary, reversibly change their viscosity. These liquid components are not to be released, even under pressure.

MAds include some natural dry clays and synthetically produced silica gels. MAbs mainly include natural bentonites, which are often modified for different applications.

Bentonites are clays and minerals containing smectite, usually montmorillonite, as well as other minerals such as mica and zeolites. In conjunction with their function as absorbents, the high swelling capacity of some of these materials is of special interest. Bentonites are also used as desiccants and, in suspension form, as materials and for products with thixotropic properties (see p. 38).

Loam has been in use as a construction material for thousands of years in various forms including stones, mortar and render for shelters and houses. By the 1920s artificial MAds were being produced. This was also around the time that silica gel was developed at the Johns Hopkins University in Baltimore, Maryland, USA. In recent years there has been an increased use of natural and synthetic zeolites, which are specially developed for today's new applications. Since 1987 bentonite in Germany has been in use in mats for sealing.

MAd materials and components in use include:

INORGANIC COMPOUNDS
Silica gels, dry clays (e.g. activated alumina, calcium bentonite, loam), molecular sieves (synthetic zeolites), gypsum.

MIXTURES INCORPORATING INORGANIC COMPOUNDS
Calcium bentonite/calcium chloride ($CaCl_2$).

ADDITIONAL COMPONENTS
Colour indicators (e.g. cobalt chloride ($CoCl_2$), methyl orange)

As there are many natural materials such as wood, paper, leather, raffia among the ranks of organic adsorbents (OAd) and they are able to adsorb only relatively small quantities of water in the form of vapour, they will not be dealt with further here. In this context it should be mentioned that the hygroscopic property of paper in conjunction with a photocatalyst is used in Japan among other places; this so-called photocatalytic paper cleans the room air of pollutants with the help of light (see titanium dioxide (TiO_2), pp. 100 ff.).

The use of mineral absorbents (MAb) to waterproof buildings has become part of the current state of the art. As they can also be used for other purposes, these smart materials will be considered only to a limited extent here. Bentonite in particular is one of these materials in which both the take-up and take-in mechanisms can occur, and therefore mineral ad- and absorbents (MAd, MAb) will be brought together in one chapter. These smart materials are classed as inorganic ad- and absorbents (IAd, IAb).

MAb materials and components in use include:

INORGANIC COMPOUNDS
Calcium bentonites (unactivated bentonites), activated bentonites (or active bentonites), natural sodium bentonites.

MIXTURES INCORPORATING INORGANIC COMPOUNDS
Bentonite mixtures.

Materials and components for the manufacture of MAds and MAbs must be able to perform through a relatively high number of cycles of exchange of gaseous or liquid components without any noticeable loss of capacity, and contain no volatile toxic substances.

The following MAds and MAbs are among those of interest in architecture:

SILICA GELS
They are made synthetically using sodium silicate and a silicic acid in various particle shapes (irregular, spherical) up to approx. 8 mm grain size and with different pore diameters. They are available in various ranges of effectiveness to achieve different air moisture contents, and can be regenerated at temperatures of +130°C to +200°C.
+ Market presence, can be made in large quantities, many years of practical use, usable over a comparatively large temperature range (ca. –30°C to +80°C), small particle size means suitability as bag fillings, uses include desiccants, moisture buffers and heat-emitting smart materials, can incorporate colour indicators, non-combustible, not sensitive to mechanical vibrations, maintenance-free.
– Relatively short replacement life (< 10 regeneration cycles), sometimes the accompanied development of heat may be undesirable, relatively large amount of dust released, relatively poor air circulation and low adsorption speed compared with spherical silica gels, will burst in direct contact with water.

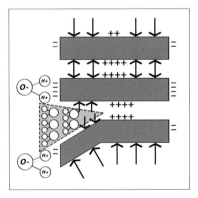

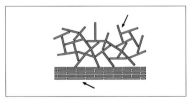

Bentonite swelling.

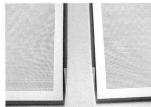

Silica gel granulate without and with indicator. | Silica gel granulate with methyl orange as indicator in unsaturated (inactive) and saturated (active) state. | Bentonite granulate. | Silica gel bags. | Gypsum wallboard with zeolite.

CALCIUM BENTONITES

Natural clay mineral, available as powder or granulate, which can be further processed in various ways, suitable for use in bentonite suspensions e.g. for sealing soil layers. They can be regenerated in the presence of air.

+ Relatively long replacement life (> 10 regeneration cycles), usable over a comparatively large temperature range (< –30°C to > +80°C), uses include desiccants, moisture buffers and seals (due to their moisture-sensitive volume change), can be processed into clay bricks or clay render among others. Otherwise as above.

– Volume changes may be undesirable for certain applications. Otherwise as for silica gels above.

ACTIVATED BENTONITES, NATURAL SODIUM BENTONITES

Clay minerals with mainly sodium ions in the intermediate layers, activated bentonites, natural sodium bentonites are used e.g. for sealing soil layers. They can be regenerated in the presence of air.

+ Relatively long replacement life (> 10 regeneration cycles), usable over a comparatively large temperature range (< –30°C to > +80°C), uses include moisture buffers and seals (due to their moisture-sensitive volume change).

– Not suitable or only suitable under certain conditions for processing into clay bricks or render.

LOAMS

Mixtures composed of various ratios of clay, sand and other components.

+ Usable over a relatively large temperature range (< –30°C to > +80°C), suitable as moisture buffers, can be processed e.g. into clay bricks or render, non-hazardous. Otherwise as for silica gels above.

– Relatively poor adsorption capacity, lower adsorption speed compared with silica gels, calcium bentonites and zeolites.

ZEOLITES

Natural and synthetic alumino-silicates with a well-defined cluster structure. Natural zeolites can be used, among others, as heat-emitting smart materials, synthetic zeolites for drying gases (e.g. air), available as powder and granulate, which can be further processed in various ways. They can be regenerated at temperatures of +250°C to +400°C or under negative pressures (evacuation).

+ Relatively long replacement life (> 10 regeneration cycles), can be used over a comparatively large temperature range (< –30°C to > 400°C) as desiccant or filtration media, catalyst for conversion of pollutant gases and as a heat-emitting smart material. Otherwise as for silica gels above.

– Relatively high regeneration temperatures required. Otherwise as for silica gels above.

As the hygroscopic effect of gypsum is well known it will not be discussed further here.

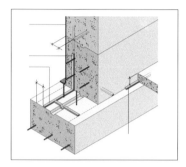

Band (strip) with MAb (bentonite). |
Installation of bands and mats with
MAb (bentonite). | Sealing effect of
mats with MAb (bentonite). | Mat
(geotextile) with MAb (bentonite).

mineral ad-/absorbents (mAd, mAb) › products

Mineral adsorbents (MAd) such as silica gels and activated alumina are used in the dehydrated state as desiccants, e.g. for the separation of gases and stored parts of water vapour. In the non-dehydrated state they are used as water vapour-sensitive moisture buffers in a number of fields, e.g. for constant air moisture content in rooms and transport containers. MAds are also used in museums, where they are found in glass display cabinets containing moisture-sensitive articles such as pictures or metal artefacts. To improve handling and for dust protection MAds are often packed in water vapour-permeable bags, and when colour indicators are incorporated at least one side of the bag is transparent or translucent to make the contents visible. Flexible tubes of foil are filled in sections with MAds and sold in strips of different lengths, either with different fillings or simply with silica gel in buildings. They are often used to prevent the growth of moulds and their spores, in particular in lightweight timber constructions that may still have a relatively high moisture content. This is done by installing several strips on the inner side of the cladding.

Mineral absorbents (MAb) are familiar as moisture and odour absorbents in cat litter; bentonite being one of them. Bentonites are also used in architecture. Calcium bentonites, activated bentonites and natural sodium bentonites are used in suspensions for their supporting and sliding properties. The latter are also incorporated into mats and panels, where they are contained in textiles or cardboard in various ways. Areas of application include hydraulic, highway, tunnel and landfill construction as well as use as seals around basement walls, joints between buildings, foundations etc. The sealing effect of these products relies on their ability to absorb relatively high volumes of aqueous components and swell to form sealing gels, which fill or close any cracks or other weak spots. The swelling pressure also fixes the products more firmly in place.

In addition to loose powdered and granulated fillings the following products incorporating MAds or MAbs are of interest in architecture:

BAGS WITH MAd FILLING
MAds enclosed in water vapour-permeable foil or paper are used to dry the air in transport containers or electronic equipment.
+ Market presence, can be made in large quantities, easy to apply, relatively little or no dust released, can be attached to or incorporated into many different types of construction, wide range of products available, resist mechanical loads and direct application of water, relatively inexpensive. Otherwise as for MAds above.
– Not universally available, approval may be required for certain applications in some countries, relatively poor air circulation and low adsorption speed compared with non-foiled MAds, the use of paper alone does not provide adequate fire resistance. Otherwise as for MAds above.

Available or developed products useful in architecture include:

RAW OR END PRODUCTS:

POWDERED MAds or MAbs (e.g. calcium bentonite)

GRANULATED MAds or MAbs (e.g. silica gel)

INTERMEDIATE OR END PRODUCTS:

BAGS with MAd fillings (e.g. calcium bentonite)

BANDS (strips) incorporating MAds or MAbs (e.g. silica gel)

GYPSUM WALLBOARDS incorporating MAds
(zeolite, in particular clinoptilolite)

MATS (boards) incorporating MAbs (e.g. natural sodium
bentonite)

PANELS incorporating MAbs (e.g. natural sodium bentonite)

STRIPS WITH MAd FILLING
MAds enclosed in water vapour-permeable foil or paper are used to dry components with residual moisture content, e.g. those made from wood.
+ Can be suspended in place. Otherwise as above and for MAds.
− As above and for MAds.

GYPSUM WALLBOARDS INCORPORATING MAd
Zeolites (in particular clinoptilolites) enclosed in gypsum wallboards are currently available in sizes 2000/3000 mm x 1200/1300 mm x 12.5 mm and can be used like conventional gypsum and fibre cement wallboards. They are especially suitable where air quality improvement by conversion and some binding of pollutant gases and unwanted odours is required, and for the adsorption of water vapour.
+ Market presence, can be made in large quantities, easy to use. Otherwise as for MAds above.
− Relatively expensive compared with conventional gypsum wallboards. Otherwise as for MAds above.

BANDS (STRIPS) INCORPORATING MAb
Bentonites (e.g. natural sodium bentonite) bound in a matrix with one side having a stabilising textile webbing and/or covered with a self-adhesive strip for attaching to a component are currently available for example in sizes 25 mm x 12 mm and 25 mm x 19 mm. They are especially suitable for sealing components in contact with earth against aqueous solutions, e.g. ground water, and are regenerated to a certain extent in the presence of air.
+ Market presence, can be made in large quantities, can be used over a comparatively large temperature range (−18°C to +80°C), easy to use, can be used where sealing by water-sensitive volume change is required, relatively long replacement life (> 10 regeneration cycles), relatively good UV resistance, non-combustible, insensitive to mechanical vibrations, maintenance-free.
− Not dimensionally stable enough for some applications, relatively low absorption speed compared with powdered MAbs and superabsorbent polymers.

Other products incorporating MAbs include:

MATS INCORPORATING MAbs
PANELS INCORPORATING MAbs

mineral ad-/absorbents (mAd, mAb) › projects

Bentonite has been the main mineral adsorbent (MAd) product in use in architecture to date. Generally it has been used in suspensions to seal layers of soil in earthworks. There are also systems of cardboard containers filled with bentonite powder or coarse granules on the market. They are used in the so-called *"braune Wanne"* or brown tank technique for sealing building basements at the external walls and in the foundation area. Any water encountered, e.g. standing ground water or water from surface water soakaways, swells the edges of the boards and any other points of weakness, and seals the system against further entry of water. Apart from calcium bentonites, stronger swelling sodium bentonites are also used. They can be classed as mineral absorbents (MAb).

Rather new on the market are multifunctional acoustic gypsum wallboards incorporating MAds, which, in addition to their inherent sound-absorbing and air moisture-buffering properties, can improve room air quality by binding and converting odours and pollutants. The first projects have already been realised using this product.

the factory

Monosmart material | Monosmart application
Gas/water-storing smart material:
GYPSUM WALLBOARDS WITH ZEOLITE
Sound absorption, air cleaning

Marco Duchow, **Alexander Duchow**, Germany
**Industrial monument with multifunctional catalytic gypsum wallboard
ceilin** | Cottbus, Germany (2005)

For its use as a call centre, the column-free hall in the roof story of the industrial monument *die fabrik* (the factory) in Cottbus had to have good room acoustics. Hamburg architects Marco and Alexander Duchow had been commissioned to give the historic room, where heavy looms once worked under a barrel roof, a more modern character without losing the aesthetic of the old factory.

Following information from a major German manufacturer about the advantages of a new type of acoustic gypsum wallboard that improves room air quality by the action of its incorporated zeolite, the decision was made to use the material for cladding the curved soffit of the roof construction.

With gypsum as the main constituent (90%) the boards have moisture-regulating properties and, because of incorporated additional layers of catalytic zeolite powder (clinoptilolite <10%), can also bind or convert various odours and pollutants. The actual physical and chemical processes involved are not fully understood at the moment. There is no possibility of pure ad- or absorption processes without the conversion of these substances taking place or of the boards becoming saturated over time.

Trials have shown that levels of cigarette smoke and the pollutants it contains (such as formaldehyde and acetaldehyde), carpet and mattress odours and the dodecene incorporated in the products, benzene from motor vehicle exhaust gases and paints, aromatic hydrocarbons in printed products and cleaning agents can be significantly lowered.

die fabrik: view at night. | View into the call centre with air-cleaning ceiling formed with curved gypsum wallboard incorporating zeolite.

absorbent/superabsorbent polymers (AP, SAP) › materials

Absorbent polymers (AP) are synthetic hydrophilic three-dimensionally cross-linked polymers that are able to take up liquid components (e.g. water, aqueous solutions, oil) on to their internal surfaces and take them into their volume, and reversibly change their volume, density and/or optical properties. These liquid components are not released, even under pressure. Modifications to long chain molecules allow these products to be adapted and optimised for a wide range of uses.

It is their ability to absorb large amounts or water and aqueous solutions very quickly that makes these products particularly interesting in the field of architecture. Currently, there are APs available that, depending on the liquid to be absorbed (the sorbent), can absorb volumes of liquid some 30 times their initial volume, in the case of deionised water 500 times, in a relatively short time. This time may be anything from a few seconds to a few minutes, depending on the type of sorbent, the quantity of the absorbing polymer granulate and the surface area/volume ratio. These materials are called superabsorbers or superabsorbent polymers (SAP).

Before SAPs were developed, cellulose was used instead; its high suction property made it useful in hygiene products, e.g. in disposable nappies. In 1986 the world's first facility for the production of SAPs was brought into operation in Germany. Since then cellulose has been increasingly replaced in suitable products by SAPs, which have also found new uses, e.g. as soil additives in agriculture. In addition to Germany, the most important manufacturing countries are the USA and Japan.

Materials and components in use include:

ORGANIC COMPOUNDS
Sodium polyacrylate

ADDITIONAL COMPONENTS
Pigments, aromatics, odour absorbers, silicates, mineral dust

Materials and components for the manufacture of APs/SAPs must in some cases be able to perform through a relatively high number of cycles of exchange of liquid components without any noticeable loss of absorption properties. Accordingly, there must be no loss of capacity and no significant reduction in speed of absorption after at least 10 cycles. As well as meeting these requirements, APs and SAPs must often be UV-stable and contain no volatile toxic components.

The following APs and SAPs could be among those of interest in architecture:

CROSS-LINKED SODIUM POLYACRYLATE
Three-dimensionally cross-linked hydrophilic polymers appropriately modified to suit their applications. Manufactured synthetically by the polymerisation of various components. They can be further processed into powders and granulates. Available for a range of applications. They can be regenerated for example by contact with still, moving and/or heated air.
+ Market presence, can be made in large quantities, many years of practical use, usable over a comparatively large temperature range (< –10°C to > +80°C), availability in small particle sizes means suitability as bag fillings e.g. as water absorbers or hydrogels that reversibly change from opaque to translucent, can be used as heat-emitting (latent heat creating) smart material, can be combined with pigments, aromatics, odour absorbers, silicates, mineral dusts, non-combustible when carrying absorbed water, insensitive to mechanical vibrations, maintenance-free.
– Some have relatively short replacement lives (< 10 regeneration cycles), some have low UV resistance, less air circulation and slower absorption speed if allowed to clump.

absorbent/superabsorbent polymers (AP, SAP) › products

The main areas of use of absorbent/superabsorbent polymers (AP/SAP) are in hygiene products and agriculture. They can be added to natural or artificial soils as a soil additive in the form of burnt expanded clay or may be the single ingredient of a synthetic soil. They can also be used to provide a nutrient subsoil. A number of products have been specially developed in this area. Further applications include their use in underwater high voltage cable installations to prevent water entry in the event of damage and in packaging. A relatively new development is a chair with SAPs incorporated into the chair back upholstery. When the chair is in use, it binds any sweat, which is later released in contact with air when the chair is not in use.

Although not developed specially for use in architecture, APs as well as SAPs can find applications in flat or slightly sloping roofs. In agriculture, composite SAPs mixed with mineral components are used as soil improvers, especially in difficult soil and climate conditions, and could be found useful in green roofs in the future.

In addition to the available performance range of powder and coarse granulate absorbents that can be further optimised by addition of other ingredients, there are various intermediate and end products available. As well as loose fillings made from powdered and granulated APs and SAPs, the main products of interest in architecture are those available as composites with other components:

Superabsorber powder made from SAP in varying states of saturation.

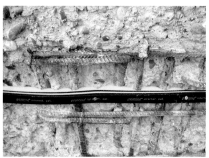

Non-composites:

HYDROCRYSTALS MADE FROM AP
Pigmented granulates of cross-linked normal absorbent polyacrylate are manufactured in almost any colour as irregular particles of up to about 4 mm grain size and used for keeping plants continuously supplied with water and in place in their containers.
+ Relatively good regeneration performance, can be installed in or on many types of construction, relatively little tendency to clump compared with powdered APs and SAPs. Otherwise very similar to cross-linked sodium polyacrylate.
− Not universally available, approval may be required for certain applications, relatively slow absorption speed compared with powdered SAPs. Otherwise very similar to cross-linked sodium polyacrylate.

SUPERABSORBER POWDER MADE FROM SAP
Fine white granulates of cross-linked superabsorbent sodium polyacrylate, irregularly shaped with a grain size of about 1 mm. Uses include the manufacture of various composites, the quick absorption of a range of liquid media (e.g. water, bodily fluids and oil) and the continuous supply of water to plants.
+ Can be used in and on various types of construction, for example textiles. Otherwise very similar to cross-linked sodium polyacrylate.
− Not universally available, approval may be required for certain applications, relatively slow desorption speed compared with absorption speed, relatively high tendency to clump compared with coarsely granulated APs and SAPs. Otherwise very similar to cross-linked sodium polyacrylate.

Technology by Rascor: compression of purple-coloured AP in a daywork joint. | Section through band composite with empty AP channel (above foam band). | Installed band composite with AP not yet compressed.

Technology by Geohumus: agro-composite incorporating SAP before swelling. | Demonstration of the swelling capacity of a compressed cube. | Plant with SAP in the root area. | Cultivation trial in a greenhouse at the Justus Liebig University, Gießen, Germany.

Composites:

BAND COMPOSITES INCORPORATING AP

Hydrogel made from polyacrylate, produced from two liquid components immediately before application; the hydrogel band, initially uncross-linked and later normally absorbent, is compressed into a hollow cell plastic profile with an additional foamed material band. Currently available with the dimensions 30 mm x 20 mm x 2000 mm. The products are used to absorb aqueous solutions and for sealing, e.g. against the entry of ground water under pressure.

+ Market presence, can be made in large quantities, can be used over a comparatively large temperature range (< –10°C to > +60°C), can be installed in or on different types of construction, can be used as a water absorber, an irreversible colour change (e.g. purple to colourless) indicates hydrogel, relatively long replacement life, maintenance-free.

– Not universally available, relatively poor absorption capacity and slow absorption speed compared with powdered SAPs.

AGRO-COMPOSITES INCORPORATING SAP (E.G. TECHNOLOGY GEOHUMUS)

Irregularly shaped composite granulates with grain sizes up to about 4 mm made from cross-linked superabsorbent sodium polyacrylate with incorporated silicates and mineral dusts. Their uses include continuously supplying water and support to plants whilst keeping the soil surface open.

+ Market presence, can be made in large quantities, can be used over a comparatively large temperature range (< –10°C to > +80°C), availability in small particle sizes means suitability as bag fillings e.g. as water absorbers and heat-emitting (latent heat creating) smart materials, relatively long replacement life (> 10 regeneration cycles), relatively good UV resistance, non-combustible, insensitive to mechanical vibrations, maintenance-free.

– Not universally available, cannot change reversibly from opaque to translucent (mineral components).

LAYER COMPOSITES INCORPORATING SAP
Irregularly shaped, fine, white granulates of cross-linked superabsorbent sodium poly-acrylate that are interlayered between textile layers, sometimes together with cellulose. Their uses include the absorption of liquids in packaging.
+ Market presence, can be made in large quantities, depending on the layer materials and SAP used they can be used over a comparatively large temperature range ($< -10°C$ to $> +80°C$), uses include water absorbers and heat-emitting (latent heat creating) smart materials, relatively good UV resistance, insensitive to mechanical vibrations, maintenance-free.
− Relatively short replacement life (< 10 regeneration cycles) depending on the layer material and SAPs used, relatively poor air circulation and slower absorption speed compared with coated APs and SAPs, may be combustible depending on the layers used.

absorbent/superabsorbent polymers (AP, SAP) › projects

Whilst superabsorbent polymers (SAP) have in a few cases been successfully used as soil additives in green roofs, other uses of absorbent polymers (AP) and SAPs in architecture are currently still insignificant. They could be used, possibly on a large scale, for difficult soils and in hot and dry climates. This would include deserts (arid zones) and in particular the cultivation and long-term support of vegetation layers. Suitable polymers could also be used to store rainwater, perhaps temporarily, and release it, when necessary, into building components in contact with inside or outside air, e.g. when the room air is too dry and/or surface temperatures are too high. It is feasible to incorporate APs and/or SAPs into wallpapers, wall coverings and room dividers, where it would be possible to install sufficiently coarse, non-woven fabric so that the granulate could be permanently contained in place even after complete absorption has occurred. Membranes, perhaps made from textiles or ETFE film, could incorporate APs and SAPs in pockets or bubbles.

Currently available or developed products relevant to architecture include:

RAW OR END PRODUCTS

FINE GRANULATES (powders) of APs, SAPs

COARSE GRANULATES (e.g. crystals) of APs, SAPs

INTERMEDIATE OR END PRODUCTS

BAND COMPOSITES incorporating APs

AGRO-COMPOSITES incorporating SAPs

LAYER COMPOSITES incorporating SAPs

FILMS incorporating APs

Hydroabsorber foils

Monosmart material | Monosmart application
Water-storing smart material:
FOILS INCORPORATING AP
Water-sensitive light transmission-changing surfaces and
building envelopes

Axel Ritter, Germany
Water-sensitive, light transmission-changing foils |
Germany (1994)

These two technology demonstrators show how APs could be
integrated into foil membranes to create light transmission
and colour changing building envelopes.

Enclosed in the hemispherical cells of an ordinary, commercially available bubble wrap, these colour-pigmented AP
granulates were tested to see if they were able to permanently change the transparency of foil membranes under the
influence of water and the hydrogels formed.

For the prototype, AP crystals were placed in the cells. Grav-
ity caused them to accumulate at the bottom of each cell
with the result that the foil remained generally transparent.
The cells were then half-filled with water to allow maximum
swelling volume. The contact with water initiated swelling in
the crystals and thus produced changes in light transmission and colour.

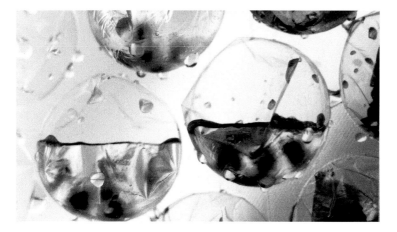

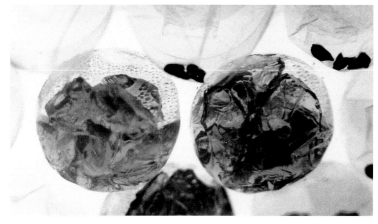

Hydroabsorber foils: detail of several cells with roughly half-
swelled crystals (semitransparent: transparent/opaque). | Several
cells, some with completely swelled and some with unswelled
crystals (semitransparent: transparent/opaque). | Several cells
with fully swelled crystals (opaque).

sources

BOOKS, MAGAZINE ARTICLES, INTERNET PUBLICATIONS

Addington, D. Michelle; Schodek, Daniel L.: *Smart Materials and Technologies for the Architecture and Design Professions*, Architectural Press/Elsevier: Oxford, 2004

Apel, Veronika; Binas, Jonathan; Gantner, Johannes; Schütz, Mark-Felix: *Neue Techniken zur Energiegewinnung – Die Nanokristalline Farbstoff-Solarzelle (Grätzel-Zelle)*, Waldorfschule Darmstadt, May 2005

Arch+ Verlag (Editor): *Material*, Arch+ 172, December 2004

Atelier Brückner (Editor): *experiment cyclebowl*, avedition, 2001

Bar-Cohen, Yoseph: *Electroactive Polymers as Artificial Muscles – Reality and Challenges*, The American Institute of Aerospace and Astronautics, Paper 2001–1492

Behrendt, Ernst: *Das Kraftwerk in der Streichholzschachtel – Thermoelemente wandeln Wärme in elektrische Energie um*, in: hobby – Das Magazin der Technik, No. 11, November 1958, pp. 41–45 & p. 164

Bletz, Michael: *Untersuchungen über das Schalten photochromer Indolinospirobenzopyrane*, Dissertation, Fachbereich Chemie und Pharmazie der Johannes Gutenberg-Universität Mainz, Mainz, 2001

Buller, Barbara: *Thermisch schaltbare Polymere eröffnen neue Anwendungsfelder*, in: Kunststoffe, 6/2006, pp. 51–53

Chan Vili, Yvonne Y. F.: *Creating Smart Textiles using Shape Memory Materials*, Heriot-Watt University, Galashiels, 2003

Dinkla, Söke: *Die Fassade als barocke Bühne?*, in: Pro Architektur, 01/97, pp. 42–44

Hill, Jonathan: *Building the Drawing*, in: Architectural Design (AD) – Design Through Making, Vol. 75, No. 4, July/August 2005, pp. 13–21

Hochkirch, Axel: *Denkmalschutz: Farbwechsel durch Mikroorganismen*, in: Kosmos, 12/92

Hummel, Hans-Ulrich; Krämer, Georg: Gips-Zeolith-Platten zur Verbesserung der Innenraumluft-Qualität, in: Zement Kalk Gips, Vol. 58; No. 11; 2005; pp. 80–86, Vol. 59; No. 01; 2006; pp. 72–80

Jendritza, Daniel J. et al.: *Technischer Einsatz Neuer Aktoren – Grundlagen, Werkstoffe, Designregeln und Anwendungsbeispiele*, 2nd ed., expert-Verlag: Renningen-Malmsheim, 1998

James Robinson: *New uses for photochromics*, in: Speciality Chemicals Magazine, October 2003

Kraft, Alexander; Rottmann, Mathias; Heckner, Karl-Heinz: *Steuerbare elektrochrome Farbfilter – Intelligente Verglasung für Fahrzeuge, Gebäude oder Displays*, in: Laser+Photonik, 1/2006, pp. 28–30

Kraft, Alexander; Rottmann, Mathias: *Intelligente Fenster und automatisch abblendbare Spiegel: Die Elechtrochromie macht's möglich*, at: http://www.aktuelle-wochenschau.de/woche13b/wochenschau13b.html, 2006

Kubisch, Christina; Leitner, Bernhard: *Zeitversetzt / Shifted in time*, Kehrer: Heidelberg, 2004

Le Corbusier: *Vers une Architecture*, Paris 1922, English edition: *Towards a new architecture*, London 1947

Lenz, Christoph: *Lumineszenz – Spektakuläre und nützliche Eigenschaften von Mineralien*, at: http://www.geoberg.de/text/geology/05111601.php

Matério (compiled): *Material World 2 – Innovative Materials for Architecture and Design*, Birkhäuser: Basel; Boston; Berlin, Frame: Amsterdam, 2006

Meyer, Bruno K.; Farangis, Baker: *Herstellung und Charakterisierung von schaltfähigen Spiegeln*, at: http://meyweb.physik.uni-giessen.de/1_Forschung/Arbeitsgebiete/Spiegel.html

Morita, Koichi; McCabe, Steven: *US-Japan Cooperative Structural Testing Research Program on Smart Structural Systems*, in: UJNR Panel on Wind and Seismic Effects – Panel Update, Vol. 1, No. 5 February 2004

Muthumani, K.; Sreekala, R.: *Structural application of smart materials*, at: http://dbtindia.nic.in/woman/paper15.htm

N.N.: *Wohnen im Grünen wörtlich genommen*, in: SKIN, May 2005, pp. 54–55

Oswalt, Philipp (Editor): *Wohltemperierte Architektur*, C.F. Müller: Heidelberg, 1994

Richardson, Thomas J.: *New Electrochromic Mirror Systems*, at: http://www.lbl.gov

Ritter, Axel: *Autovariable nonenergetische Gebäudemembransysteme*, Seminar Report, Universität Stuttgart, Summer Semester 1994

Ritter, Axel: *„Es" bewegt sich – Reagible Tragstruktur aus Glasfaserkunststoff*, in: AIT Spezial – intelligente Architektur, No. 4, 03/96, pp. 70–71

Ritter, Axel: *Flexible Tragstruktur aus Glasfaserkunststoff*, in: Arch+, 12/95, p. 136

Ritter, Axel: *Polyreagible Mechanomembran mit wettersensibler Ausstattung – Lektionen aus der Natur*, in: Intelligente Architektur, No. 36, 09–10 2002, ch. 16

Roth, Werner; Schilz, Jürgen; Steinhüser, Andreas: *Thermoelektrische Wandler als Zusatzstromerzeuger*, Forschungsverbund Sonnenenergie „Themen 96/97", pp. 77–83

Saße, Dörte: *Photochromes Glas erstmals umweltfreundlich hergestellt*, at: http://www.wissenschaft.de/wissen/news/151511.html

Schmitt, Michael: *Entwicklung dotierter und undotierter Nb_2O_5 Sol-Gel-Schichten zur Anwendung als färbende Elektrode in elektrochromen Systemen*, Dissertation, Technische Fakultät der Universität des Saarlandes, Institut für Neue Materialien gem. GmbH, Saarbrücken, 1999

Schulz, Bernd (Editor): *Felix Hess – Light as air*, Kehrer: Heidelberg, 2001

Shor, Shirley: *Smart House – Version 2.0 – Das Haus von Bill Gates als Modell für das Haus der Zukunft*; at: http://www.heise.de/tp/r4/artikel/6/6255/1.html

Stöger, Christian: *Hightech-Textilien aus Spinnenfäden*, at: http://www.expeditionzone.com/story_detail.cfm?story_id=2723

Tagawa, Kikuko: *Light + bright fabrics – Photocatalyst technology has come a long way, and it's adding value to fabric in surprising ways*, in: Industrial Fabric Products Review, January 2005, pp. 30–35

Toepfer, Wolfgang: *77 Meter hoch und ganz in Grün: der "Monte Verde" in Wien*, in: Stein, Keramik, Sanitär, No. 5, 2005, pp. 8–10

van Onna, Edwin: *Material World – Innovative Structures and Finishes for Interiors*, Birkhäuser: Basel; Boston; Berlin, Frame: Amsterdam, 2003

White, Mary Anne; LeBlanc, Monique: *Thermochromism in Commercial Products*, in: Journal of Chemical Education, Vol. 76, No. 9, September 1999, pp. 1201–1205

Wortmann, Arthur: *Game Boy*, in: Mark 1 – Let's Build Trees, Architecture comes alive, No. 01, Winter 2005/2006, pp. 50–65

CATALOGUES, WHITE PAPERS, BROCHURES

Dehnstoffarbeitselemente mit PTC; company publication by
  Behr Thermot-tronic GmbH, Kornwestheim

EunSook Lee, catalogue of exhibition at Republic of Korea
  Embassy, 26 November to 5 December 2003, Berlin

*Förderpreis zum 3. Studentenwettbewerb „Textile Strukturen
  für neues Bauen 1995"*, white paper published by
  Techtextil-Symposium, Arbeitskreis Textile Architektur
  und der Messe Frankfurt,1995, Frankfurt

Gelsenkirchen-Stiftung (Editor): *Kinetische Kunst – Die
  Sammlung des Städtischen Museums Gelsenkirchen*,
  Edition Braus: Heidelberg, 1998

*GLASSX verwandelt die Glasfassade in ein Klimatisierungse-
  lement mit nachhaltiger Energiebilanz*, company
  publication by GlassX AG, Zurich, Switzerland

Heckner, Karl-Heinz: *Intelligente Gläser im Energiemanage-
  ment von Gebäuden – Fenster mit variablen optischen und
  thermischen Eigenschaften*, in: conference paper at
  „GLAS" – Innovationsforum für Glasvarianten, Haus der
  Technik, Berlin, on 03.06.1999

Nitz, Peter: *Sonnenschutz mit thermotropen Schichten*,
  white paper for the 1st Leobener Symposium Polymeric
  Solar Materials, Leoben, 2003

*Optimal gekoppelt: Akustik und Raumluftqualität – Call
  Center im Industriedenkmal „die Fabrik" in Cottbus*, press
  release by Knauf Gips KG, Iphofen, 2005

Piezokeramische Materialien und Bauelemente, company
  publication by PI Ceramic GmbH, Lederhose, Germany

Sigmar Polke, catalogue of exhibition at Musée d´Art
  Moderne de la Ville de Paris, ARC, Paris, from 20 October
  to 31 December 1988

SmartWrap; company publication by KieranTimberlake
  Associates, 2003

*Thermobimetalle – Grundlagen, Berechnungen, Gestaltung,
  Auswahl*; company publication by G. Rau GmbH,
  Pforzheim, 1989

Toyoda, Hiroshi; Nakata, Takayuki; Abe, Kazuhiro:
  *Photocatalytic properties of membrane materials treated
  with titanium dioxide for architectural membrane
  structures*, company publication by Taiyo Kogyo Corp.,
  Osaka, Japan

Verbundprojekte, in: Ergebnisse aus Forschung und
  Entwicklung, ZAE Bayern, 2003, pp. 48–53

*Wie das Auge in der Bleistiftzeichnung herumspaziert, so
  meldet das Hirn...*, leaflet by Ruth Handschin about the
  light installation at Künstlerhaus Bethanien, Berlin, 1990

INFORMATION SOURCES ON THE INTERNET

http://www.art-site.de/ruth.handschin
http://www.autonomic.uiuc.edu

http://www.bayermaterialscience.de
http://www.bine.info
http://www.chempage.de
http://www.dyesol.com
http://www.eamex.co.jp
http://www.e-ink.com
http://www.el-licht.de
http://www.el-technik.de
http://www.emfit.com
http://www.empa.ch
http://www.enocean.com
http://www.functionalpolymers.basf.com
http://www.innovations-report.de
http://www.inhaus-duisburg.de
http://www.ise.fhg.de
http://www.oled.at
http://www.photochromics.co.uk
http://www.privalite.com
http://www.rinspeed.com
http://www.sam-tetec.com
http://www.seilnacht.com
http://www.storelite.com
http://www.tagesleuchtfarben.ch
http://www.tii.se/static.htm
http://www2.uni-jena.de/chemie/institute/oc/weiss.htm
http://www.we-make-money-not-art.com
http://wikipedia.org

UNIVERSITIES, INSTITUTIONS

Eidgenössische Materialprüfungs- und Forschungsanstalt
  (EMPA), Dübendorf

Forschungszentrum Jülich (FZ Jülich), Jülich

Fraunhofer Institut Angewandte Polymerforschung (IAP),
  Potsdam-Golm

Fraunhofer Institut für Solare Energiesysteme (ISE),
  Freiburg

Fraunhofer Technologie Entwicklungsgruppe (TEG),
  Stuttgart

Philipps-Universität, Marburg

Technische Universität Berlin, Physikalische und Theo-
  retische Chemie, Berlin

Universität des Saarlandes, Fachbereich Organische
  Chemie, Saarbrücken

LECTURES ON THE SUBJECT BY THE AUTHOR

*Häuser mit IQ – Die smarten Eigenschaften des Wassers als
  Auslöser komplexer Veränderungen am Haus*, invited
  lecture to the 3rd Students' Congress at the Fachhochschule Suderburg, 05.06.1994

*Sich verändernde Häuser als Ergebnis biologischer Prozesse
  auf Natursteinflächen*, invited lecture to the 4th Students'
  Congress at the Fachhochschule Nürtingen, 14.05.1995

Gewichtsgesteuerte Phänomene, invited lecture at the
  Institut für leichte Flächentragwerke (IL) of the Universität Stuttgart as part of an international symposium,
  28.05.1998

Smarte Materialien für eine neue Architektur, invited lecture
  at the Fachhochschule Koblenz, 09.06.2004

PUBLICATIONS RELEVANT TO THE SUBJECT BY THE AUTHOR

Airship hangar wins textiles design prize, publication of a
  design for a pneumatically convertible airship hangar
  with a bivalent load bearing structure – Luftschiffhalle
  Friedrichshafen, in: Technical Textiles International,
  November 1995

Airship hangar designed with textile structure, publication
  of a design for a pneumatically convertible airship
  hangar with a bivalent load bearing structure – Luftschiffhalle Friedrichshafen, in: High Performance Textiles,
  November 1995

Publication of a design for a pneumatically convertible
  airship hangar with a bivalent load bearing structure –
  Luftschiffhalle Friedrichshafen, in: Techtextil-Telegramm,
  December 1995

A pneumatic convertible, publication of a design for a
  pneumatically convertible airship hangar with a bivalent
  load bearing structure – Luftschiffhalle Friedrichshafen,
  in: fabrics & architecture, 01–02 1995

Dreilagige Textilhülle von 157 m Länge, publication of a
  design for a pneumatically convertible airship hangar
  with a bivalent load bearing structure, in: Techniker-
  Magazin, June 1995

Publication of a design for a weight-controlled building by
  the Kinetic Design Group at the Massachusetts Institute
  of Technology (MIT), at: http://kdg.mit.edu/Matrix/
  matrix.html, since December 1999

Publication of a design for a reactive mechanical membrane, in: Wallpaper*, December 2002

Publication of a competition design for a building with a
  reactive mechanical facade capable of changing its
  textural and light transmission properties, by: Exhibition
  by the Aufsichts- und Dienstleistungsdirektion Trier at the
  Elector's Palace, Trier; Exhibition by the Verbandsge-
  meinde Verwaltung Hermeskeil, Hermeskeil, October
  2003

NOTES ON THE TEXT

[1] http://kdg.mit.edu/Matrix/matrix.html

[2] Hofmeister, Sabine: *Der beabsichtigte Zufall und die gewollten Veränderungen im malerischen Werk Sigmar Polkes*, Diplomarbeit, Institut für Technologie der Malerei, Stuttgart, May 1993

[3] van Hees, Rob: *Laboratory Profile: Conservation Techniques*, at: http://www.tudelft.nl/~

[4] E-mail from Herbert Enzler, technical assistant at the Institut für Polymerwerkstoffe und Kunststofftechnik of the TU Clausthal dated 14.11.2005

[5] Schmidt-Mende, P.: Aktoren mit Formgedächtnislegierungen, in: Jendritza, Daniel J. et al.: *Technischer Einsatz Neuer Aktoren – Grundlagen, Werkstoffe, Designregeln und Anwendungsbeispiele*, 2nd ed., expert-Verlag: Renningen-Malmsheim, 1998

[6] E-mail from Dipl. Masch.-Ing. ETH Patrick Lochmatter, Eidgenössische Materialprüfungs- und Forschungsanstalt (EMPA), Dübendorf dated 22.06.2006

[7] Bouas-Laurent, H.; Dürr, H.: *Organic Photochromism*, in: Angewandte Chemie, No. 116, 2004, pp. 3404–3418

[8] *Helioseal Clear Chroma – farbverändernd, transparent, ästhetisch*, company publication by Ivoclar Vivadent AG, Schaan, Lichtenstein

[9] Stephan, Jörg: *Beitrag zum Greifen von Textilien*, *Dissertation*, Fachbereich 11 Maschinenbau und Produktionstechnik der Technischen Universität Berlin, Berlin, February 2001

[10] *Keramische Fliesen mit Hydrotect Oberflächen-Veredelung*, company publication by the Deutsche Steinzeug Cremer & Breuer AG, Bonn

[11] Blasse, Grabmeier, 1994

[12] Mann, Martin: *… und es leuchten die Wände*, in: hobby – Das Magazin der Technik, No. 8, August 1957, pp. 74–77

[13] Elektronik, 12/2002

ILLUSTRATION CREDITS

AGROB BUCHTAL: 99 top, 106, 107 (photos: Pez Hejduk)

© Alsa: 82, 85

© Anja-Natalie Richter: 64

© atelier brückner: 13, 14 top (all photos: Thomas Mayer)

© Autostadt: 14 bottom

© Axel Ritter: 11 left (photos: Axel Ritter); 15, 46 top (graphic: Axel Ritter); 52 (graphic: Axel Ritter); 57, 58 (photos: Axel Ritter); 76 left 1st, 2nd and 3rd from top; 81; 91; 100; 113 (photo: Axel Ritter); 162, 163 (photos: Axel Ritter); 174 (photo: Axel Ritter); 177 2nd from top (photo: Axel Ritter); 183; 187 (photos: Axel Ritter)

© BASF: 165; 167 left, right 1st from top; 170

Bayer: 20 2nd and 3rd from top

© Behr Thermot-tronik: 49, 50

© BMW Group: 21 right

© Bryan Boyer: 46 bottom; 71

© Bugatti: 16

© Christina Kubisch: 116

© Christopher Glaister, Afshin Mehin, Tomas Rosen: 88

© CLOUD 9 (Enric Ruiz Geli): 128; 129

© 2006 Cute Circuit: 18; 20 1st from top

© DaimlerChrysler: 21 left 4th from top

© Daniel Pelosi: 41 3rd and 4th from top

dECOi Architects: 12

© Deutsche Steinzeug Cremer & Breuer: 101; 102; 104 1st from top

© DieMount: 126 left 3rd from top, right 1st from top

© Ewald Dörken AG: 166 2nd and 3rd from top; 167 right 2nd from top

© Dyesol: 144 1., 2nd and 3rd from top; 145; 147

© EADS: 62

east Hamburg: 104 4th from top

Eike Becker Architekten: 78

© E Ink / Citizen: 93 1st from top

© E Ink / LG.Philips LCD: 93 2nd from top

© E Ink / Polymer Vision: 93 3rd from top

© E Ink / Toppan Printing: 95 right 1st from top

© Emfit: 155 3rd from top; 158 1st and 2nd from top

© EMPA: 66; 67; 68; 69

© EnOcean: 158 3rd from top

© EunSook Lee: 110 bottom; 117

© European Bioplastics: 30 1st from above (photo: Treofan), 2nd from above (photo: Novamont)

© Felix Hess: 161

© FerroTec: 152 3rd from top

© Fludicon GmbH: 38 left 1st from top, right

© Fraunhofer IAP: 83 (photos: Armin Okulla); 84 (photo: Armin Okulla); 138 (photo: Armin Okulla)

© Fraunhofer ISE: 76 right; 77; 144 4th from top; 146

© Fraunhofer TEG: 149 3rd from top

Freihofer: 29 left 2nd from top, right 1st and 2nd from top

© FZ Jülich: 155 1st from top

© 2006 G+B pronova: 32 right

© Geohumus International: 185

© Gesimat: 92 1st and 4th from top; 95 left 1st from top

© GKD / ag4: 127 right

© GlassX: 164 (photo: Gaston Wicky); 166 1st from top (photo: GlassX); 168 (photo and graphics: GlassX); 171, 172 (photos: Gaston Wicky)

© G. Rau: 53; p. 54; 55; 56; 61

© Gruppe RE (Silke Warchold, Nicole Hüttner): 23 right (photos: Lucas Roth); 119 2nd and 3rd from top (photos: Sabrina Rothe)

© Grado Zero Espace: 17, 19 left 1st, 2nd and 4th from top

© Hannaliisa Hailahti: 124

hobby – Das Magazin der Technik, No. 8, August 1957, 74, 75 and 77: 132 1st and 2nd from top

hobby – Das Magazin der Technik, No. 11, November 1958, 164: 153

© Jaithan Kochar: 42 right 2nd and 3rd from top

© James Robinson: 74 1st and 2nd from top; 75

© KieranTimberlake Ass.: 140; 141

© Knauf Gips: 177 right 2nd from top (photo: Albert Weisflog); 181 (photos: Albert Weisflog)

© J. Mayer H.: 72 (photo: Uwe Walter); 87

© Juliet Quintero: 123

Kowa / Kirakira-Komichi: 120; 121 top

Kowa / Mamoru Nanba: 119 1st from top

© LBL: 92 2nd and 3rd from top

© LBM: 40

© Lichtpapier (Anke Neumann): 114 1st and 2nd from top (photos: Anke Neumann); 121 2nd and 3rd from top (photos: Anke Neumann); 132 3rd and 4th from top

lif Germany: 127 left 3rd from top

© Loop.pH (Rachel Wingfield, Mathias Gmachl): 133; 134

© 2004–2006 Lord Corp.: 38 left 2nd, 3rd and 4th from top

© 2006 LUMINEX: 23 left

© Merck: 31

© 2006 Messe Frankfurt Exhibition GmbH: 19 left 3rd from top (photo: Jean-Luc Valentin); 20 2nd from top (photo: Jean-Luc Valentin)

© 2006 Michael Bleyenberg: 34; 35

© Micropelt: 151; 152 1st from top

© Minimax: 48 2nd and 3rd from top

© Mirow Systemtechnik: 157

© Mitchell Joachim: 11 right

Mitchell Joachim, Lara Greden, Whitney Jade Foutz, Wendy Meguro, Luis Rafael Berrios-Negron: 142; 160

© National Museum of Emerging Science and Innovation: 39

© NAUE: 178 4th from top

© 2006 NO-CONTACT (Adam Whiton, Yolita Nugent): 19 right

© Norbulb Sprinkler Elemente: 48

© Novaled: 135 top; 136; 137 1st and 2nd from top; 139 2nd and 3rd from top

© OKER-Chemie: 177 left 1st and 3rd from top, right 1st from top

© 2004 Olafur Eliasson: 33

© Osram Opto Semiconductors: 126 left 1st 2nd and 4th from top, right 2nd from top; 135 bottom; 137 3rd from top; 139 1st from top

© Permalight: 118 1st from top

© Peter Linnett, Tobi Blunt: 51

© Peter Marino Architects: 96 left; 97 right

© Peter Yeadon: 42 left, right 1st from top

© Philipps-Universität / N. Hampp: 74 3rd and 4th from top; 76 left, 4th and 5th from top

© PI Ceramic: 154; 155 2nd from top; 156

© Prinz Optics: 32 left

© Rascor International: 184

© RC TRITEC: 111 top; 112; 118 2nd and 3rd from top

© Rinspeed: 21 left 1st 2nd and 3rd from top

© RPM/Belgium N.V.: 176; 178 1st, 2nd and 3rd from top

© R&Sie... (François Roche): 10

© Ruth Handschin: 110 top; 114 3rd from top; 115; 122

© SAM – Span and Mayrhofer: 149 left, 1st and 2nd from top, right 1st and 2nd from top; 152 4th from top

© SCTB NORD: 152 2nd from top

© SensiTile Systems: 37

© SGG: 94; 95 left 2nd from top, right 2nd from top; 96 right; 97 left; 103

© 2006 Sharon M. Louden, courtesy of the Artist and Oliver Kamm/5BE Gallery: 25

© SHARP: 41 2nd from top

Sigmar Polke: 24; 86

Solitech – Innovative Solartechnik: 127

© Taiyo: 104 2nd and 3rd from top

© Taiyo / Obayashi Corp.: 99 bottom; 105

Technische Universität Berlin / G. Hauck: 80

© Interactive Institute / Front design: 79

© Interactive Institute: 22

© UIUC: 28

wikimedia.org: 59; 98; 111 bottom; 150

© Würth Solar / Universität der Künste Berlin: 41 1st from top

© Yvonne Chan Vili: 65

© Zigan Displays: 130